BEYOND TOUCH SITES:

An Anthology of the Tangible

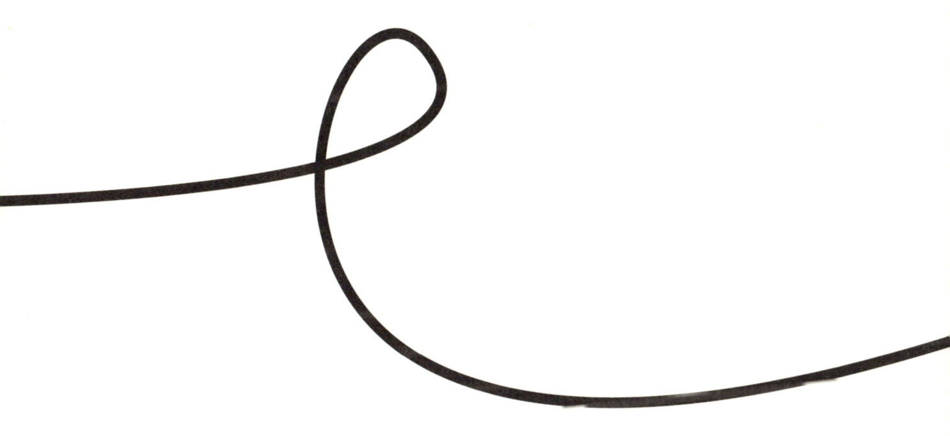

Edited by
Wendy McGrath

Copyeditor
Shelagh Kubish

Beyond Touch Sites: An Anthology of the Tangible
Editor: Wendy McGrath
Copyeditor: Shelagh Kubish

Cover and book design by Cecilia Salcedo

Library and Archives Canada Cataloguing in Publication

Title: Beyond touch sites : an anthology of the tangible / edited by Wendy McGrath.
Names: McGrath, Wendy, editor.
Description: Includes bibliographical references and index.
Identifiers: Canadiana 20240496752 | ISBN 9781777085964 (softcover)
Subjects: LCSH: Touch–Literary collections. | CSH: Canadian literature (English)–21st century. | LCGFT: Literature.

Classification: LCC PS8237.T67 B49 2025 | DDC C810.8/0353–dc23

ISBN 978-1-7770859-6-4

Printed and bound in Canada

Laberinto Press Ltd.
7407-119 Street NW
Edmonton, AB T6G 1W2
Canada

www.laberintopress.com

“So much time is spent releasing light from graves, holding the flame as it flutters in our cupped hands.”

- Beatriz Hausner, *She Who Lies Above*

Contents

Editorial Team

Luciana Erregue-Sacchi

Luciana Erregue-Sacchi is the Director of Laberinto Press. She lives in Edmonton, Alberta, with her husband, Mauricio. Luciana misses the hugs of her children, already out in the world, and those of her near and dear, back in her native Argentina.

Wendy McGrath

Wendy McGrath, a Métis poet, writer, and artist living in amiskwacîwâskahikan (Edmonton), is the winner of the inaugural Prairie Grindstone Prize. McGrath's writing embraces multiple genres. Her most recent publication, *The Orange Scribbler* (JackPine Press 2023), is a chapbook/artist's book inspired by heirloom recipes. She has collaborated with visual artists and musicians, exploring the relationships between genres. Her latest collaboration, *The Beauty of Vultures* (forthcoming NeWest Press 2025), is a poetry collection inspired by and including the bird/wildlife photography of Danny Miles, drummer for the band July Talk.

McGrath has published four novels, two poetry collections, and two chapbooks/artist's books which explore a range of forms and approaches. *Broke City*, the final book in her Santa Rosa Trilogy, continues her exploration of the prairie gothic. She is a board member of NeWest Press.

Shelagh Kubish

Shelagh Kubish has worked as a book editor in Edmonton, both in-house and freelance, for many years and enjoys taking books in various genres through to publication. She also has edited and written for magazines and taught grammar and editing in post-secondary and professional settings.

Note from the Publisher

“Remember here in Canada, we keep the equivalent of an arm’s distance from each other,” the ESL instructor cheerfully told the class at UBC International House. It was 1992, and I was refreshing my conversational English. Memories of a bearded guy in my town, a musician, who hugged and was hugged by everyone while he waited for the bus, offered a much-needed contrast as I was unable to reach out to my loved ones in Argentina, except through collect phone calls and once-a-year visits. Once I settled in Canada, the poetry of Leonard Cohen offered a world of tactile possibilities, as in his song “Suzanne,” in which he describes the ultimate tactile experience–touching others’ bodies with our minds. After 2020, the sense of touch has been guilty, innocent, virtual, splintered, as we make up for lost time. It is in this AI, fake-versus-real, convoluted present that Laberinto Press’s fourth anthology emerges–thanks to the editing talent of Wendy McGrath, the keen eye of our copyeditor, Shelagh Kubish, and the innovative design ideas of Cecilia Salcedo. It has been a dream to work with all of them. With acute sensibility, Wendy has harnessed the many touch sites proposed by the contributors and made this volume THE ultimate tactile map, where multi-genre narratives expand and contract, sit in haptic dialogue next to each other, in the hopes of touching their audience with this collection’s beating heart.

Luciana Erregue-Sacchi
Publisher
Laberinto Press

Introduction

When I accepted Luciana Erregue-Sacchi's invitation to edit this anthology, I was excited by the theme: touch. I felt this one-syllable word offered real, surreal, and ethereal possibilities for contributors. And as I reviewed submissions, I was astonished by how these writers approached "touch" in such unique ways, working in multiple genres and incorporating multiple languages.

Editing *Beyond Touch Sites: An Anthology of the Tangible* was an experience that allowed me to inhabit the liminal space between genre, time, place, and life and death.

One of the things I like most about working with other writers is what I learn from them. As I worked on this anthology, I found my sense of touch, both literal and figurative, moved beyond everyday definitions. I am sure readers of this collection will find it just as transcendent.

Wendy McGrath
Editor

Foreword

From the moment we leave the warm seas of our mothers' bellies to join the world of Alone, tactility defines the contours of our being. With smell, touch is the oldest of our senses. It is also, as the explorations in *Beyond Touch Sites: An Anthology of the Tangible* reveal, one of the most complex and intimate conduits of human experience and communication.

All-enveloping as our skin, our haptic sense can localize, lightning-quick, to specific memory sites. Prismatic and often paradoxical in meaning, "touch is a bridge," as Uchechukwu Peter Umezurike writes. Touch can heal and harm, comfort and confront, catalyzing the other senses and carrying us to distant places. Touch moves us. We are touched.

The modalities of touch addressed by the authors in this collection range across a spectrum of forms of contact: reparative, violent, retributive, gustatory, familial, ritual and ceremonial. From feeling "the intention behind a touch," in Rona Altrow's phrase, to tracing its ripple effects into the present and the future, touch is a temporal event that unfolds in unexpected and often gripping ways in the stories, poems, essays, and hybrid experimental and performative scripts collected here.

Assembling original work in (mostly) English by emerging new voices and established writers who challenge the boundaries of touch, *Beyond Touch Sites: An Anthology of the Tangible* features writing that simultaneously challenges literary, generic, linguistic and cultural boundaries. In measuring the invisible radium of touch, the authors gathered in this collection integrate the work of translation and cultural crossings, enriching our understanding of corporeal experience with new layers and nuance. *Beyond Touch Sites* takes us on migrations both physical and imaginative.

The journeys here transport and transform.

Christine Wiesenthal, PhD
Professor Emeritus
Department of English and Film Studies
University of Alberta

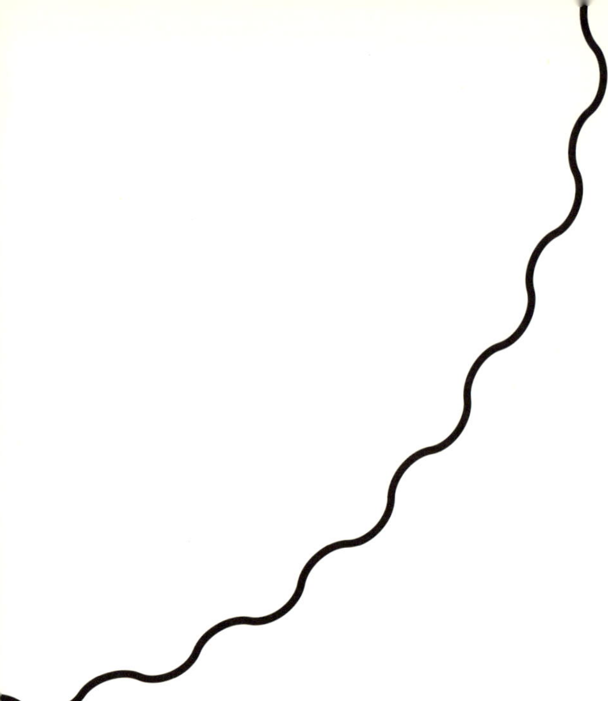

TENDER

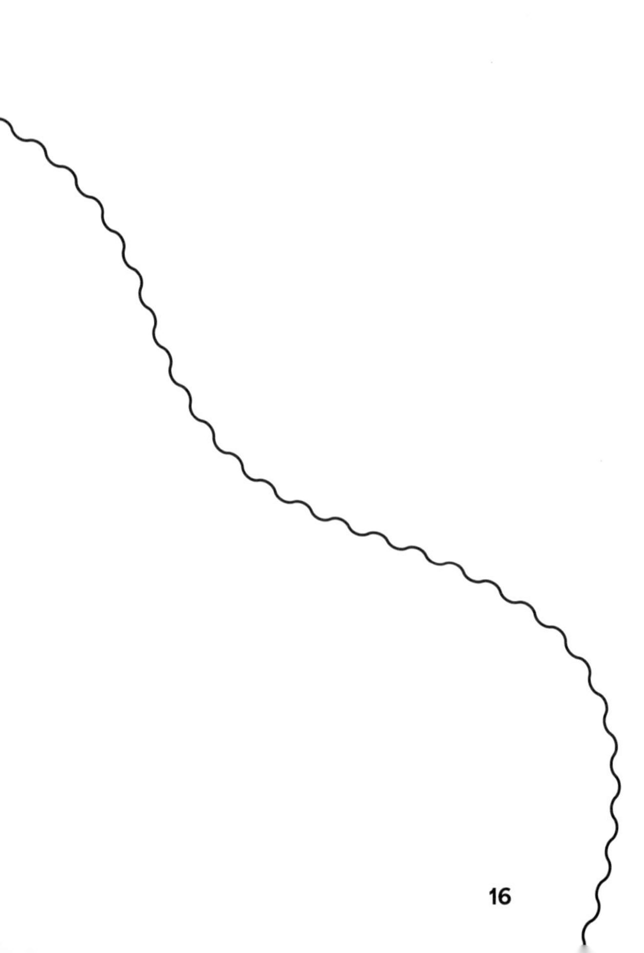

How to Handle Oversized Dreams Gently Despite the Violence Coating a Weary Body

by Medgine Mathurin

Begin with your knees
Kiss them
Each limb that survived
Pull closer to your heart
They carried you
Thank them for surviving war

Let each eye swell and leak
Witness your own baptism
Palms up, face heading sunset,
Make a nest out of your hands
Braid every finger together
Gently, the way your mother weaved your kinky hair
To keep you from wailing
You, tender-headed
Child
Build your own cradle
Lay your head there
Joy is a fruit that ripens in the dark

Close your blinds
Teach your pupils to stop searching for answers
Should you require assistance,
Consult your chest
Let every subtle crest
and fall
remind you of the steadiness of sunrise

Bury beneath
your own
melancholy
fogging each lung
unsung promises

Lie

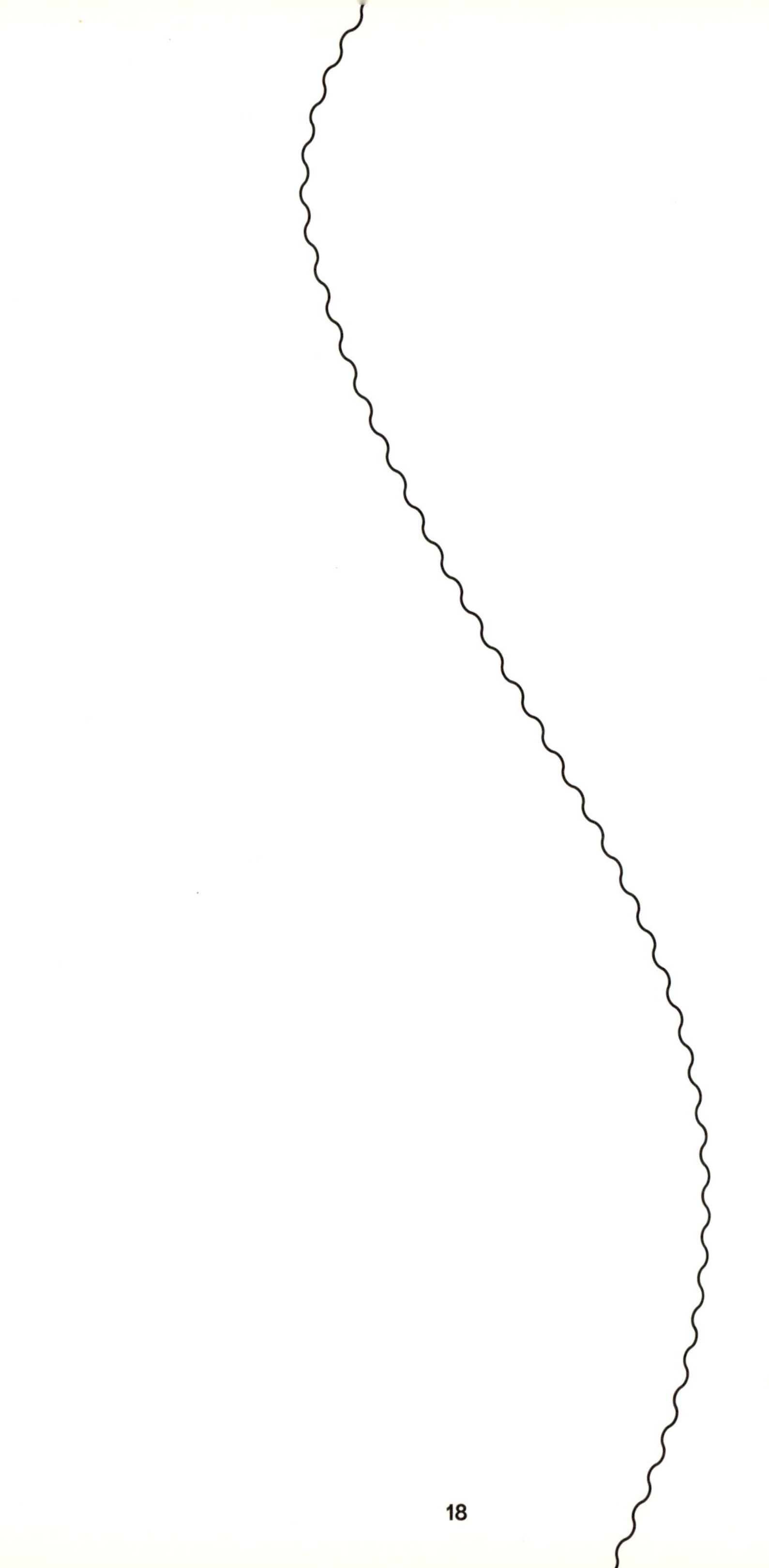

Aftercare

by Medgine Mathurin

I pored over aftercare instructions
Found no recipe to make a balm to recover
Every punctured vein, ego, and ambition

No water to help me swallow the bitter of my new slow
No supervision for prednisone night sweats
No warning to clear my agenda indefinitely
No medical script to soothe the lonely of ribs and limbs
No contingency plan for the heavy
No gauze for the tender

They missed it

Again

Only the swelling of eyelids
Only discharge papers

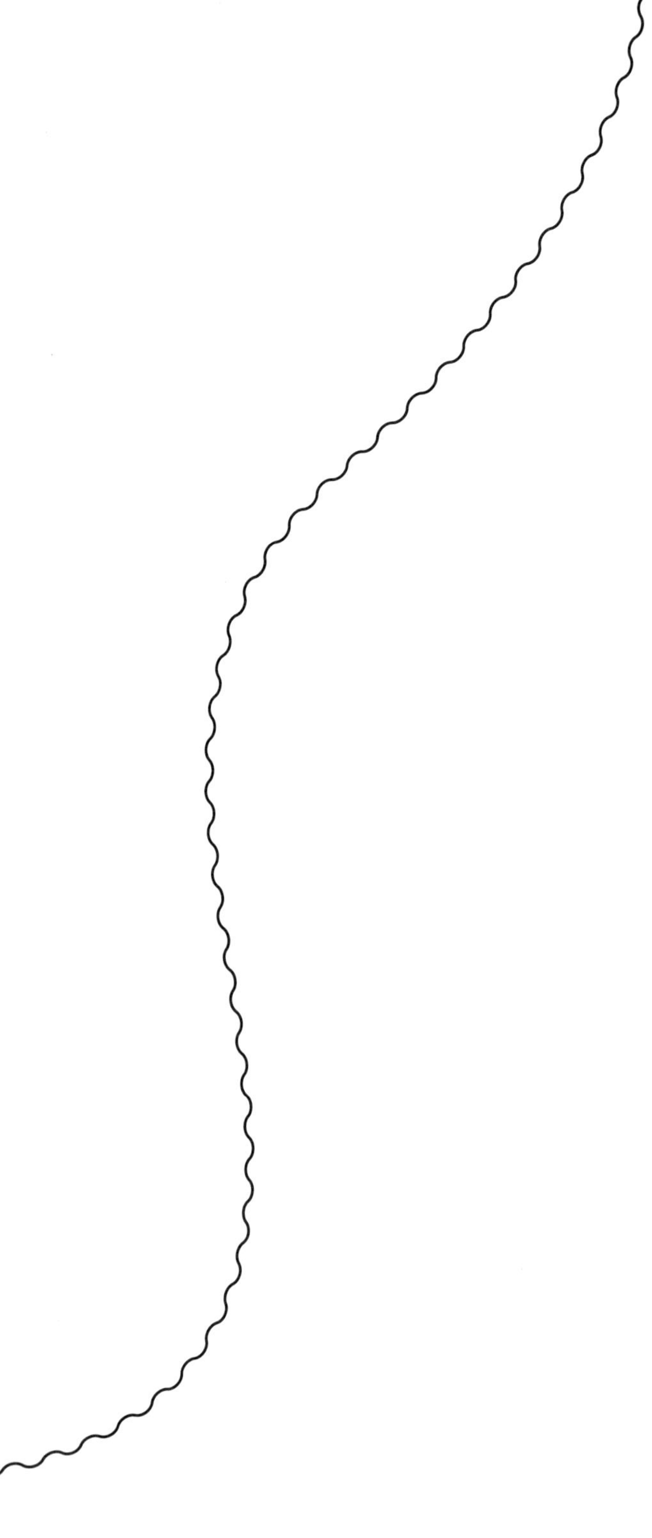

Lost and Found: My Story About Fatherhood

by Sandro Silva

My one-year-old son is already playing the pandeiro, a Brazilian hand drum that looks and sounds like a tambourine. In our kitchen, I sing a samba song to him while I rhythmically tap the pandeiro in my hand. He giggles and spins with excitement, and then walks over to playfully grab the instrument from me. I pick up a shaker and start to play it. Smiling as he paces back and forth, he holds the pandeiro in one hand and hits it with the other. It barely makes a sound as his tiny hand touches the thinly stretched leather covering the drum's wooden frame. He squeals with happiness and flashes his nearly toothless grin. He's energized and moves closer, looking up to make eye contact with me. I carry on singing and playing the shaker. Suddenly he stops. The drum goes rolling down the hallway. He's done. I hold on to these moments of spontaneous joy, etching them into my memory. Sometimes, I record them on my phone and share them with friends and family in Brazil or elsewhere. Everybody is so impressed by my son's ability to quickly learn the joys of samba. I guess babies can learn anything.

We might not remember facts or details from the early stage of our lives and yet this proves to be the most important time to build a foundation for life. I think of my own father, his short presence in my early life, losing him to a long absence, and then finding him as I began my own journey of fatherhood, touch my life, here, now.

•

When I think about my father, I immediately switch to memories of my mother. I'm not exactly sure how my parents met, but I know he started living with my mother in our family home when she already had two young sons by two different men, neither of whom was anywhere to be found. A few years later I was born, the first of three children my parents shared.

Our tiny shack sat at the top of the hill of Jardim Monte Azul, which dipped down into a deep valley on the outskirts of São Paulo. The main road wrapped around the favela and led to nearly desolate places in all directions. The road was unpaved reddish-brown dirt. It had once been fertile, green land for farming, but unofficial settlements–favelas–started to dot the area as more people came to the city for a better life.

People like my father made the arduous trek from northeastern Brazil as drought ravaged the Sertão, the hot and dry backlands. Some people were starving to death, and for many Afro-Brazilians who were still out working the land, coming to São Paulo to work for wealthy white families in the industrial hub proved to be better than waiting for rain that did not come.

For my parents, the land of new opportunity proved stressful and suffocating. We were never meant to thrive in the city. We were just meant to serve the people allowed to thrive. And as our family grew from two to five kids, the fragile walls of our one-room shack felt like they were closing in on us. The tension in the air could be felt at home. My dad's temper would often boil over and explode. At times it felt safer to be out in the uncertain streets than in the house. My parents never married. Breaking up was as simple as walking out the door and not coming back. That's exactly what my father did.

With little opportunity afforded to us favelados, many young men and boys in the favela resorted to drug trafficking to make a living. The drugs came with guns, and violence quickly started to rule. My mom didn't want us, her children, to become part of the statistics. For a little while, my dad would stop by, but eventually he moved to a different neighbourhood. The visits became less frequent. And then he moved even farther out of the city and stopped visiting altogether. At this point, it was the late 1980s. My mom had another child by another man who didn't stay, and five kids at home became six. Her small salary working as a maid wasn't enough to provide for all of us as hyperinflation decimated the economy.
When the holes in my clothes grew larger, she would push me to go visit my father to ask for money. I was old enough, she'd say. With all the stops, the journey on a single bus would take well over an hour. It was an uncomfortable and exhausting trip. And I had to get off at the very last stop. I hated going there, especially on Saturday mornings.

Not long after, my father, who'd had enough of city life, moved with his new wife to a small town. It was in the neighbouring state of Minas Gerais, where two of my favourite authors, João Guimaraes Rosa and Carlos Drummond de Andrade, my mom, and Pelé, the king of soccer, were born. At the time, our stopping by for a visit would have been the only way for him to see his children. But we didn't see him anymore. The next time I saw him was almost a decade later. And I was the only one from home to visit him. My two young sisters didn't have any further contact with him.

Eventually, I went to law school. I was one of three black students and the only one from a favela. During the five-year degree program, one of the other black students switched to morning classes and the other paused for a semester due to financial issues. I'm not sure if they graduated. I did. The university I attended was my second choice. My days were long. I would step outside at 7 a.m. to work all day in the mailroom at a law firm that also helped with my tuition. I'd take classes in the evenings and get home just before midnight. Weekends were often consumed by studying and some leisure playing soccer on Sunday mornings. By my early 20s, I was already burnt out and I hadn't even started my career as a lawyer.

But I thought reconnecting with my father after a lost decade would be therapeutic, now that I was well on my way to earning my living.

Through our community, my mother found out that he had relocated with his new wife to Santa Helena de Minas, a tiny town with just a few thousand residents. Via our networks, I let him know that I was coming for a week-long visit. I bought a bus ticket and began the long trek up to rural Minas Gerais.

My journey started at Tietê Bus Terminal–the world's second-largest bus terminal after New York City's Port Authority. The terminal had been built by nordestinos like my father. It was for the people who helped build São Paulo into the mega-metropolis it was, and who served it every day. The terminal was bustling, full of people coming and going. Based on the people I saw there, it seemed like many nordestinos were trying to visit loved ones in remote parts of the country. Some people travelled with thin, recycled plastic bags that doubled as luggage.

I hopped on my first bus to Belo Horizonte, the capital of Minas Gerais state. I'd then have to connect to another and then another to get to my final destination. The lengthy journey gave me nearly 30 hours to read and think. I barely slept. I didn't know what to expect either. I no longer needed my father's money, I was just a bit nervous.

As I brought up memories of my father from my early years, I couldn't find a single image or event to suggest we were close. We had never shown any affection towards each other. I was told to obey and was not supposed to be the curious kid inquiring about everything. My mom never went to school. She had to work instead. My father never stayed in school for longer than a semester. At the age of six he was already fighting for survival with his father pushing him to his limits. He rarely mentioned his father, my grandpa, who apparently could be violent toward his kids. Brutality and punishment were passed down through generations.

Every time I was severely punished, I'd hear, "If not here, someone else will punish you out there, and that will be even worse." My parents would agree on that. But my father was a strong man who didn't have to do much to hurt me. I never understood why he came home late at night, with reddish eyes, slightly limping, speaking too loud while exhaling cheap alcohol. Furious against the world. We had to pay for it should my mom dare to inquire as to his whereabouts. Time and again I would make the mistake of staying out to play street soccer with other kids until after dark. My punishment would be visible on my back for days.

Somehow, we were always in danger and literally anything could happen to anyone when the sunlight reached the other side of the globe, leaving us in darkness. "Quando o dia escurece só quem é de lá sabe o que acontece" (when nighttime arrives, only people from the favela know what happens there), sang our neighbours' hip hop band Racionais MCs in the early '90s, in their brilliant denunciation of the happenings in the favelas.[1] A 2012 *New York Times* opinion article noted that the United Nations once named the neighbourhood of Jardim Ângela "the most dangerous on earth."[2]

By the time they were 10, most kids from the favelas had already seen a dead body on the streets. My parents feared that one of us could be part of this daunting statistic of young black males dying. We're beyond vulnerable. It might sound contradictory, but my father was trying to keep me away from any extra danger perpetrated by the police or bandits. Or both. Still, I didn't like to be physically hurt to learn any lesson. And I know, now, that I wasn't an angel either.

•

When I finally arrived at his new home, my father was waiting for me at the bus stop, which was identified simply by a wooden stump on the side of the road. Slumped over and standing barely taller than the stump itself, he had certainly aged since the last time I saw him.

He still had a full head of black hair, but his black skin looked more lined and leathered. We didn't cry or hug each other then. At first glance, it looked like I'd travelled to the past. I felt a little unsettled by that. The region was among the poorest in Brazil. Forgotten by the mainstream and hurt by the effects

---

1 The Racionais MC. "Pânico na zona sul." *Holocausto Urbano*. Zimbabwe Records, 1992. LP.

2 Willis, Graham Denyer. https://www.nytimes.com/2012/12/02/opinion/sunday/in-brazil-poverty-is-deadly-for-police-officers.html December 1, 2012.

of all sorts of lack of infrastructure, from open air sewage heavily polluting the nearest river to being hours away from any social service in case of an emergency. It's a tiny city after all, it doesn't need everything, one might say, but that place also felt the impact of issues affecting bigger cities. A few people manipulating the money to benefit only a handful of families didn't bring any progress to the region. Many people were living below the poverty line. But they seemed content. I was seeing what I had learned from books.

We walked to my father's small bungalow. It was simply and neatly furnished. In the kitchen, his partner had placed a thermos of freshly brewed coffee and two cream-coloured ceramic coffee cups on top of a white lace doily in the middle of the table. Right next to the thermos was a plate of warm sugar cookies. Everything was set up for hours-long conversation, which was supposed to compensate for the years apart.

We began to sip our coffee and chew on our cookies, and we didn't stop until the sun went down. I was hesitant to share too much. My love of soccer, literature, and samba didn't fall in line with his new values learned from the Bible. Yes, he happily shared, he was a changed man who had "found God," and who had given up drinking. Now, going to the nearby evangelical church had become an obsession. He asked questions that suggested he was proud I was in law school. But after a while the tiredness hit me. I passed out in the next room on a clean bed carefully prepared for my stay. I was only woken up early the next morning by the noisy roosters in the neighbourhood.

Over the next week, my father would proudly present me around town to all his friends. I visited the local radio station and was even introduced to the mayor. With his chest puffed out and holding his head high, my father would pat my chest and tell everyone I was his son who was becoming a lawyer. I didn't quite enjoy the attention as all I'd wanted in that town was to be as anonymous as I was in downtown São Paulo. But once the introductions had been made, I didn't let anybody steal any more son-and-dad time. At night time, I especially appreciated how magical the skies are in rural Brazil. And before going to bed I'd spend long minutes outside his place contemplating the universe with my naked eye.

After we'd had a week together, I felt better about the metaphorically–and literally–bumpy journey that had gotten us to where we were, and I accepted that I had gotten to where I was despite not having a father figure at home. When it came time to leave, we hugged. I got on the bus, took my seat, and waved at my father from the window. Little did I know the next time we'd speak would be more than two decades later.

•

As the COVID-19 pandemic engulfed the world, I had time to reflect on my past and wanted to reconnect with my roots. I started to look for my father. It had been 22 years since my visit with him when I was in law school. My mom was no longer alive.

By this point, I had started a new life for myself in Canada. I contacted my younger sister in Brazil to help me out with the search and finally find out if our father was still alive. The quest began. We reached out to people who might have seen him. We started posting on social media pages. We even contacted a TV producer in the region where he was supposedly living. Even though social media is now omnipresent in our world, with my dad's generation in Brazil, old-school TV is how people connect. A show in his region is specifically set up for people looking for long-lost loved ones. Despite all the memories we hadn't built over our years apart, I was, once again, excited at the prospect of finding him.

Back in the spring of 2022, I got a WhatsApp voice message from my sister: she had found our dad! I remember the message. Full of excitement, she first stuttered and mumbled words and sentences and it took me a minute to fully understand the details.

When I got the news, my wife was eight months pregnant with our first child. A wave of emotions came over me. Slowly, my dad and I started to connect through WhatsApp video chats. He had spent his scarce money to buy a smartphone for the first time, just to learn the basics and interact with us remotely. It felt like we were strangers just getting to know each other after a lifetime apart. Sometimes, we'd run out of dry conversation.

Not long after my father and I reconnected, my son was born. I was there, getting ready to record the entire scene on my phone, my heart pounding inside my chest. I could hear its beat accelerate more and more until our son arrived in this world. I put my phone down and cut the umbilical cord. The tenderness in the energy exchanged at that moment weighed a soul. His first sounds touched my heart as we were already on the same rhythm. I could feel that our baby wanted to be here with us too. He couldn't wait to experience life. He arrived right on time, 12 minutes before the end of his due date.

I didn't want to sleep that night at the hospital. I was thinking deeply about everything and nothing, drawing no conclusions at all, remembering the magical moment that had taken place before my eyes. It felt extra good. Scary too. My wife and I were proud new parents. The morning after my son's birth, I video called my dad from the hospital in Edmonton. I couldn't wait to show him his grandson. I flashed the camera towards my son, wrapped in a white swaddle and white knitted hat as he slept in the sterile plastic bassinet.

I wrote dozens of unfinished poems for my son, but no words could adequately describe the silence when I was feeding him a bottle. I gently pressed his small body against mine a little longer, so we could feel each other's hearts before I put him to sleep in his crib. That calmed him down. And those shared moments melted my heart every time.

I became an expert at changing diapers. For those first months after my son's birth, I barely slept two or three straight hours a night. I never thought I was capable of learning lullabies to play on the ukulele to please him, but I did. Those days when everything seems to upset your baby, when nothing you do changes the mood, the frustration, the crying for reasons new parents have no clue how to fix, and you desperately go on the internet for a million possible answers, those endless days you wish regrets about parenting never crossed your mind, those days are hard. They drain your energy to zero and you are in survival mode. I aged years within weeks. My baby face disappeared, and I am hesitant to admit I spotted white hair on my rather distinct afro. The silver lining is that I gave up drinking alcohol altogether to look after my son, though it is something I should have done a long time ago. My mom would be proud of my decision. She knew that babies are huge responsibilities that some fathers will never understand. Now, as the primary caregiver for my son, I can't imagine what it would be like to be apart from him. I still can't process how my single mother dealt with six kids.

Two weeks after my son was born it was my father's 70th birthday. I called to wish him a happy birthday and so he could see his grandson. Calling felt nice, the right thing to do. Two weeks after that it was my birthday. My father didn't call me or message me. Nada. I was disappointed, confused, angry. But I felt I should avoid an argument.

He cold-called me days later while I was changing my son's diaper. With a wet wipe in one hand, a diaper in the other, and a crying baby in front of me, I just couldn't pick up the call. A few days later he called again and I told him I hadn't been able to pick up the previous call because I was changing the baby's diaper. Then he went mute. The look on his face in the video said, "*That's the mother's job.*" I repeated that I'd been changing a diaper, and, suddenly, there wasn't much else to say.

My father and I are still in contact. Sharing audio and videos via WhatsApp brings us joy. We are lucky enough to have found each other after a long time and now he can also contact my sisters. I hadn't had an accurate answer regarding my father's whereabouts for far too long. I was certain I'd never see him again. Year after year filling out paperwork and answering unpleasant questions have finally come to an end. He is no longer merely a name on my birth certificate. And I was the only one of his three kids to carry his name on my legal documents.

We both know now that the last call will eventually happen. Or he could disappear again at any given moment by just blocking my number. I hope that doesn't happen. Now that the baby is up and walking, our video calls are more manageable. I shared with my father a video of my son's first birthday celebration at daycare. Our son is sharing a table with a few other kids, thrilled to wear his colourful birthday hat, not knowing what's going on or why everybody else is singing and staring at him. He is clearly enjoying his first birthday cake and claps his hands to celebrate his special day.

I had hoped for a comment from my father. But, again, nothing. I respect and understand he is not particularly a tech-savvy person. Or there might be some other reason he did not respond. I understand. At this point, I am dealing with someone I don't know. Perhaps I am selfishly sending videos and voice messages expecting immediate reactions that might not arrive quickly, if ever. I understand. I really do. I just don't like how it makes me feel. But that doesn't matter.

My father was lost to me for many years, and I found him again just as I was finding my own way into fatherhood. Life evolves in ways I will never fully comprehend and, sometimes, what is lost and what is found is something beyond touch.

Finger Memories

by Jumoke Verissimo

1. Kitchen Philosophy

Eight (or nine or ten, it doesn't matter),
but the warmth of the kitchen, the ladle's familiar clink,
still fit together.
Mom cooks, her back curved by the stove's red glow. I prance around, a helper eager for a role.

I am hoping mom would ask me at some point if I'd like to make myself useful.

When she doesn't ask, I lean close to her and offer her help.

Finally, a nod, a task, a pot set bare. "Pepper, salt, and fish," she instructs with care. I bring them all, then, with a hopeful grin, offer the fermented locust beans, their wrinkled skin.

"Not for this soup," she says, a smile on her face. "Locusts can grace a dish, but here they'd run mad. A scent too strong, unwanted, it stains, a perfect creation becomes the cook's own disappointment."

I pick one, then two, then three of the locust beans and wonder about the taste I can't forget; that tangy bite, a flavour I hold close.

Mom seals the jar, a shield against the strong aroma. Then she pops a bean in,
a knowing, fleeting dusk.

"The same ingredient can bless a dish, or bring despair," she says,
"It's all about the place, the when, the loving care."

2. Butterfly Wings

A little girl is running around the park trying
to make a butterfly perch on her palm.

The butterfly is an exhibition of tenderness

with rainbows patterned on its glitter of grey
  yet sparkling wing that's blue against the sun.

I am watching the poor thing small thing as it   dips
to evade a child's delight, it glides from bloom to leaf
            shimmering lights   hunted or fancied, one can't tell.

The butterfly gets caught in a thornbush.

I leave the park, a whisper on my tongue
"tattered wings can fly too, broken songs are songs too."

My wonder lingers on in my mind:
Are gentle fingers meant to tear a silken dream or cradle beauty in a sunlit gleam?
            Is the thorn the only fear in place

3. Touching Laughter (For Vivian)

My friend's laughter arrived from the other side of the ocean.
I could touch it. I felt her rippling cheeks in my hands.
At the bus stop even as engines thrummed anxieties
into passers-by. Even as the wind bullied my joint to speak aches–

I departed the house with an ounce of hope.
Past morning squawk on a grey morning from my balcony,
past the folded throw blanket drooping down a sofa,
past the wet towel, the unfinished roast beef, and the
broken vacuum–
I arrived at the bus stop waiting for laughter I hoped to return to.

My phone rests silent in my winter jacket, a weight in winter's hold
A silent prayer for a text message delivering a surgeon's
gentle grace.

I let my hand feel everything about my friend's peachy laugh.
Soft–   *if you hold too hard it'll bruise.*
(But I do not know how else to hold laughter slipping from
my hand).

It is cold. I feel a frail silence, like humans have been evicted
from dreamy Edmonton, where skies lavish sunshine in crocheted clouds
and hide a banditry of black-capped chickadees in the deepest winter.

Led by the hand, a delicate enamelled floor of ice
glides my feet to the redolent condolences of a willow tree–
its enduring knowledge and intimacies of the roadside
bearing witness to the solemn memories of a migrant's past.
When the text comes in, I do not read it and keep holding her laughter.

I hold the tree. I do not fall. I hope the tree feels her laughter too.

4. This is How I Remember You
(For Eva)

i

A chuckle slips through your lips and I join in.
 Clean those glasses, it looks like a smoke temple.

ii

 A palpitating voice but a steady hand
 with the firmness of a tree stem.

 Water is rushing from the tap.
Our stories gush into the sink with the liquid.
 You adjust your pink winter jacket.
 Are you ready, now?

iii.

 A minivan that feels like home.
 Smells like meatballs and beet soup and turkey–grrrrrilled turkey.
 I have some food for you and J.

iv.

Here's a small book for the daughter, she'd like this.
Texting, messaging, sending email.

v.

A card signed, *Always here, Eva.*
How I hold on.

5. Ewedu Sundays

Before I learnt the English name for ewedu was jute leaves or learnt to pronounce Corchorus olitorius in science class so, it almost sounded like the refrain of pop hits that don't last, ewedu was just punishment in stalks and leaves, a chore on Sundays, before the family feast.

Once grandma arrived, laden with goodies to unpack, out came the ewedu, punishment on legs. Bunches piled on laps, a metal bowl by side.

We'd pluck and pluck, a never-ending stream, enough, Dad joked, to feed all Lagos, it would seem. (Though Lagos meant just Dad, Mom, and our brothers two, and anyone else with "lucky feet" who wandered through.)

I used to wonder if my grandma bought the market dry, or did she order ewedu mountains, enough for lifetimes fed? Since we were about to feed my family and the rest of the city it always seemed like the leaf plucking was never going to end. Pluck, pick, shed, pluck, pick, shed, pluck, shed, pick, drop, pick, drop–frustrations beat.

I suffered through it in silence, grumbling over my inflamed fingers.

But my brother who seemed to enjoy plucking leaves from the ewedu stems boasted of how he alone filled the ground with bare peduncles and whittled leaves.

He revelled in his work, a leaf-grabber extraordinaire, earning promises of meat, a reward beyond compare. While I dreamt of vanishing, of world without this green, promising myself never to eat it, this slimy, spirogyra scene.

But then, the aroma filled the air, a fragrant, savory smell, and with a sheepish grin, I reached for more, the taste a familiar well.

•

In Edmonton's embrace, a different life unfolds, motherhood's joys and challenges seek old stories.

My daughter, a stranger to Grandma's Sunday feasts. She doesn't know the patience ewedu plucking tests. But a craving for home stirs, whispers in my soul, a yearning for that familiar thing.

"What is the English name for ewedu," I search online, before my mission into this foreign space: grocery stores, produce aisles, determined, at crab-like pace.

We embark on a quest, a mission for green, searching for ewedu, a childhood scene. Online whispers lead me, store by store, down aisles of plenty, yet wanting more.

No verdant bundles just puzzled looks from store clerks I meet, until a name sparks recognition, a smile, a gesture sweet. "Check the frozen section," he directs, and there it sits, an icy slab, leaves only, no stems to pluck, a convenience I should grab.

Gratitude for convenience, a sigh escapes, no inflamed fingers. But as I look at my daughter, a strange feeling takes hold, a longing not for ewedu, but for those fingers, inflamed.

TRACE

Poses

by Catalina Morales Velez

"Jere, I am home."

I put my laptop case on the floor and hung up my purse while removing my shoes at the entrance.

"Pspsps," I called to her, but silence was all I got back.

"Jere. Pspsps...I am hooome."

A thin, elegant, green-eyed, greyish fluff showed up, walking slowly down the carpeted stairs, looking at me with her forever serious face.

"Hi, hermosa (beautiful). I am home."

She stopped at the last step before touching the hardwood floor. I looked at her and was already in love for the millionth time. She looked back at me, not moving an inch. I stepped inside, approaching the stairs. I paused around a metre in front of her and, lovingly, kneeled before my queen.

"Here, here," I said. She looked at my hand and then back at me. I waited patiently.

This is one of the best moments of the day.

Jere seemed to reconsider, and in an act of profound love–I am sure of it–she put one of her paws on the floor and started walking towards me, soon rubbing her delicate body against my thighs. A subtle purse of my lips showed on my face, and with that warmth within, I grabbed her, put my arms around her tiny body, gave her a ton of kisses, and promptly put her down.

She shook herself–too much human touch, I guess. She looked at me and walked away.

Cats are like that. They like humans, but don't get too close. They care about you, but are brutally honest about your pros and cons. It's an I-like-you-but-from-afar situation, that I confess, I kind of understand.

"How was your day?" I asked her, standing up.

"Mine was just fine," I answered her as if she had asked the question back. "Less draining than usual. Camille, though, was having one of those days."

I started to walk towards the kitchen to get a cup of tea going.
"Life is so freaking complicated, Jere. I wish I were more like you."

I looked at her, already in charge of the sofa, licking her paws while the last rays of the sun offered a golden light that was almost exclusively warming up the spot she had conquered and illuminating her radiantly.

"Yeah, something like that!" I said, enjoying, for a few seconds, the movie-like scene in front of my eyes. But then, I quickly remembered the perfectly stale reality that surrounded me.

If I could only...be...the monologue running in my head was interrupted by the buzzing of my phone. I looked around and couldn't see it, but soon tracked the sound back to my purse, which was still hanging from the knob.

"Who could that be, Jere? I doubt Camille is in the mood."

I started digging into my purse, trying to find my phone. Brzzt. Brzzt. Brzzt.

"Found it!"

I stared at the screen and saw my mother's name.

"Hola Madre, ¿cómo estás?" (Hi, mother. How are you?)

"Natico, te encontré. ¿Cómo te fue hoy? ¿Ya llegaste a la casa?" (Natico, I found you. How was your day? You already arrived home?)

"Sí, señora. Acabe de entrar. Me fue muy bien madre mía, gracias. ¿Cómo estás tú?" (Yes ma'am. I just got in. It went very well mother, thank you. How are you?)

"Pensándote." (Thinking of you.)

"Yo también mami, mucho." (Me too mom, a lot.)

"¿Ya comiste?" (You already ate?)

"No, madre. Acabé de llegar y estaba saludando a Jere." (No, mother. I just came in, and I was saying hi to Jere.)

"Ay, qué linda. Te espero todo el día, probablemente. ¿Le diste mil besos de parte mía?" (How cute. She probably waited for you all day. Did you give her a thousand kisses from me?)

"Todos los días, madre." (Every day, mother.) I answered, knowing that she meant it literally.

Jere, Mom, and I had lived together until just before I moved to Canada. Her eyes watered when I told her that I would be travelling with Jere, moving away, but at the same time, she was overjoyed knowing I would be taking Jere with me on this northern adventure.

"Tan hermosa. Me hace tanta falta." (So beautiful. I miss her so much.)

"Lo sé, madre. Ella me acompaña y cuida, tal como tú." (I know, mother. She accompanies me and takes care of me, just like you.)

"Sí, sí." (Yes, yes.) Mom thought for a few seconds and continued, "Quería saber cómo te había ido hoy." (I wanted to know how your day had been.)

"Muy bien, madre. El canal está creciendo y hay mucho trabajo pero estoy muy bien. Mis compañeros son súper queridos, mi jefe está contento, y hasta almorcé con Camille hoy." (Very good, mother. The channel is growing, and there is a lot of work to do, but I am doing very well. My colleagues are super nice, my boss is happy, and I even had lunch with Camille today.)

"Qué bien, qué bien. Saludes a Camille. ¿Le has dicho que aquí hay siempre un hogar que la espera?" (That's good, that's good. Greetings to Camille. Have you told her that there is always a home waiting for her here?)

"Claro, madre. Algún día la llevaré conmigo a visitarte. Ya verás." (Of course, mother. One day I will take her with me to visit you. You will see.)

"¿Y ya está muy frío?" (And it's already very cold?)

"No madre, tranquila. Estamos en otoño y a pesar de que aquí no dura poco, aún están los árboles bonitos. Amarillos, así como a ti te gusta. Esta época del año me recuerda mucho los guayacans del lado de la casa." (No mother, no worries. It is autumn here, and although it does not last long, the trees are still beautiful. Yellow, just the way you like it. This time of the year reminds me a lot of the guayacans on the side of the house.)

"¡Ay, sí! Algunos florecen y se ponen amarillos en noviembre." (Right. Some of them bloom and turn yellow in November.)

"Exacto." (Exactly.)

"¿Ya vas a cocinar la cena?" (Are you going to cook dinner yet?)

"No sé. No tengo mucha hambre." (I don't know. I'm not very hungry.)

"Nata," she said sharply.

"Sí, señora." (Yes, ma'am.) I answered, paying attention.

"Tienes que comer." (You have to eat.) she said demandingly.

"Sí, madre." (Yes, mother.) I responded while closing my eyes and circling my neck in readiness for the sermon.

"¿Qué vas a comer?" (What are you going to eat?)

"Mmm. No sé, madre." (Hmm. I don't know, mother.)

"¡Natalia!"

"Sí, madre, yo sé. Espera." (Yes mother, I know. Wait.) I responded heading back to the kitchen. "Mira, tengo huevos, cebolla, jamón..." (Look, I have eggs, onion, ham...) I continued my imaginary mental scan of the fridge.

"También tengo leche y sé que todavía hay chocolate en polvo. Además, tengo sopita de tomate y un poco de arroz del fin de semana. Madre, tengo comida. Yo voy a comer. ¿Quieres hacer videollamada?" (I also have milk, and I know there is still cocoa powder. Plus, I have tomato soup and some rice from the weekend. Mother, I have food. I am going to eat. Do you want to do a video call?)

"No, está bien. Ya se está haciendo tarde y tengo que ir a dar la vuelta con Lucho. ¿Me prometes que vas a comer?" (No, it's okay. It's already getting late, and I have to go out for a walk with Lucho. Do you promise me that you will eat?)

"Sí, señora. Te amo, madre mía." (Yes ma'am. I love you mom.)

"Yo a ti, Natico. Que la Virgen te acompañe." (I love you too, Natico. May the virgin be with you.)

"A ti también, mami. Un beso." (You too, mommy. A kiss.) The call ended; I stared at my phone and sighed.

"Mom really worries, Jere."

I raised my gaze and found her with her eyes closed, receiving the last sun rays on her face, making her fur appear bluish. I sighed again with envy of a cat's capacity to ease through life.

"Do you want to eat something?" I opened the fridge.

The light coming from inside illuminated nearly the entire kitchen, which was already darkening with the progressive departure of the sun.

"We have...well, not much," I said, looking at the cat food can with its cute smiley yellow cap slightly crooked, two tomatoes, butter, a half consumed container of olives, and an open package of rye bread I bought a week ago.

"What do you say, Jere? Rye toast?" I looked back to see her curling into a ball and giving me her back.

"I guess you liked rye bread as much as I did."

I grabbed her wet food and closed the door. Lifting off the yellow lid made her ears pop up.

"Yes, food time, hermosa." (beautiful)

The last of the wet food landed with its gluey fluid in her bowl, and she was immediately all over the chicken pâté. I watched her enjoy for a while and then sat down on the floor beside her. Her face, lost in her favourite flavour, reminded me of when I used to enjoy food.

"I know. Delicioso, right?" (delicious) She is so her. No filters, no expectations. She doesn't like it, she leaves it; she likes it, and she totally embraces it.

"I had lunch with Camille today. That was a nice break from work."

No stopping whatsoever from her. Only a quick shift of her head when the food got too close to her overgrown tooth.

"Jere, I am not like you. I know how to do what I do, but honestly, I don't like it. Marketing stopped being exciting a while back. I even wonder if it ever was. I am so tired. You know what's the worst part? It's not even body tired. I don't want to go to sleep." Yes, you do! "I don't want to go to the gym either." True, you are lazy as fuck. "I should do some yoga, at least." No expectation here. "But I don't want to do yoga either."

I stretched out on the floor. Jere glanced at me for a second; our eyes met, and she went back to her food.

"I have to buy some groceries. Yak. That involves talking to more people. Wow, I am sick of people, too? I am such a bad human being!" I howled and hunched, hugging my knees.

The sound of Jere's tag crashing against the bowl signalled she was licking the bottom of it–she was almost done. I unravelled into a corpse pose and closed my eyes, getting ready for her next move. If she was full, that was it for the day, but if she wanted a snack, we would have nose-to-nose contact, and I was going to feel her whiskers on my face, telling me she deserved some Temptations.

I waited.

Slowly, I opened one of my eyes to check on her and found her staring at me. Interesting.

"What's wrong, hermosa?" (beautiful) I rolled to face her, resting my head on my folded arm. Jere broke eye contact and moved on.

"I guess you are full," I said, watching her conquer my bed.
My quest, on the other hand, seemed more daunting. The unreachable fulfillment kept me lying there, feeling empty...all over again.

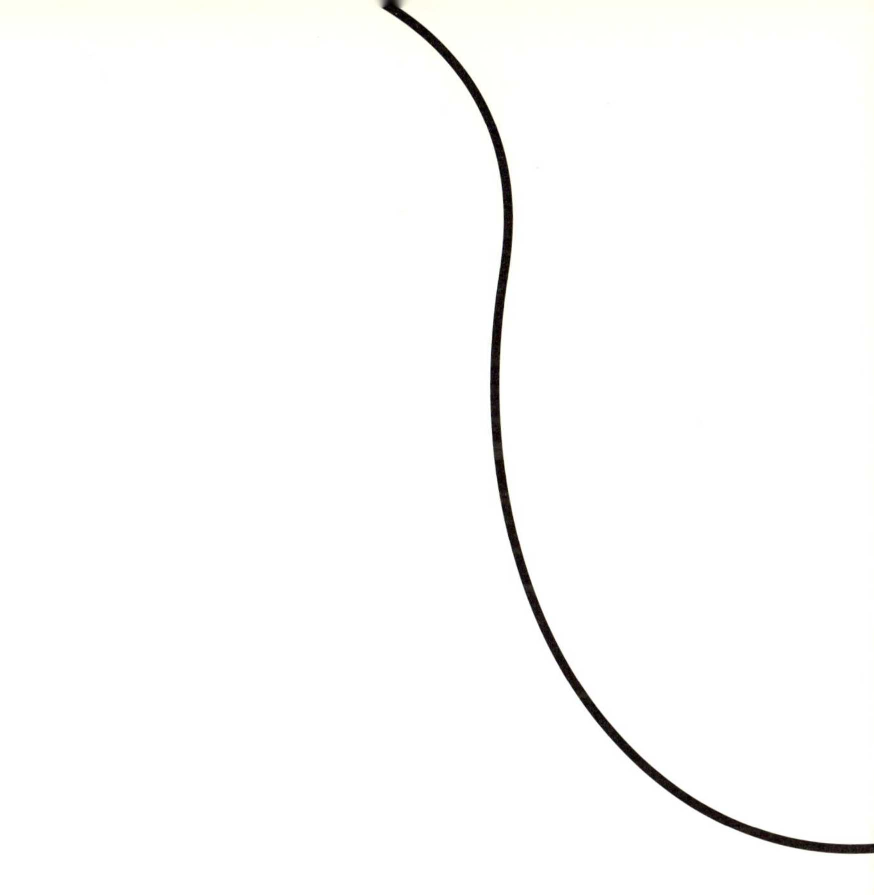

Trembles - Trembling Aspens

by Pierrette Requier

Texte pour la scene. Voix accompagnées d'improvisations de flûte ou accordéon ou violon.
A performance piece. Voices accompanied by flute/accordion/violin improvisations.

Voix intergénérationelles/Intergenerational voices
Le vent/The wind
Poète/Poet
Mémère/Grandmother
Pépère/Grandfather
Pionnières/Pioneer Women
Mères des années 1950/Women of the 1950s
Gossipy Voix/Gossipy Voice
Voix d'hommes pionniers/Pioneer Men's Voices
Voix d'hommes/Male voices
Fonctionnaire du gouvernement/Government Official
Prêtre/Priest

Flûte/Flute ou accordéon, ou violon: évoquant « le grand vide des plaines canadiennes » au début du 20e siècle : l'immensité, le vent dans les feuilles de trembles, dans les herbes hautes. Fond de chagrin, inquiétude. Longs hivers. Terres à défricher...[1]

<Musique improvisée/Music improvisations>

LE VENT:
Et le vent, et le vent, se vante à ciel ouvert...Icite, toujours le vent vente!

---

[1] Les deux langues se parlent dans un dialecte franco albertain du *The Last Best Ouest*, une region du Nord de l'Alberta. Intergenerational. Voices speak in a bilingual northern Alberta dialect spoken by francophones who came to settle that particular area.

POÈTE:
Fille du vent et
femme de ville,
je suis hantée
par la vastitude
d'où j'origine.

J'ai appris deux langues à la fois–
mes deux langues affectives se parlent constament.
Sans l'une ou l'autre, I am not whole!

PIONNIÈRES:
On se souvient de nos débuts iccite nous autres...On a recommencé à zéro.

MALE VOICE - GOVERNMENT OFFICIAL:
That this house place itself on record as being opposed to Bilingualism in any form in the school system of Alberta, and in favour of the English Language being **the only language permitted to be used as the medium of instruction in the schools of Alberta**, subject to the provisions of any law now in force in the Province in that effect.[2]

POÈTE:
Dès leurs débuts, ici dans l'Ouest,
les langues maternelles...Autres que l'anglais–
Stumped! Gone limp.
Mots échappés, tongues other than English, OTHER-ED!
Words scattered every which way.
Lost, like dust in the wind!
Ils se sont refait une langue qui fittait plusse icite!

LE VENT:
Et le vent, le vent souffle. Éparpille les mots...En sème de nouveaux!

POÈTE:
Sudden break of crow's black cry
against white bruise of sun,
veiled behind slow shifting clouds.
Here   mourning has no weight,
grief   no bearings   nor place to moor.

---

[2] Levasseur-Ouimet, France. D'année en année de 1959 à 2000, Edmonton, Alberta, Faculté Saint-Jean, l'Institut du patrimoine, 2003, p. 157 et 158.

PIONNIÈRES:
Reommencer à zéro! Aborder ce Nord, sans sentier, sans repères?

PRÊTRE:
Allez Ouest! Allez settler l'Ouest...
Y'a là des terres pour pas cher!

LE VENT:
In her ears a breath, a breath, a breath,
Surfacing just above the soil.
In her mouth a hum, a hum, a hum...

POÈTE:
Le souffle de mes défunts vibre
Au-dessus de la couche d'humus,
Couche-Vie de la terre qui nous soutient.
D'où nous provient toute nourriture.

LE VENT:
The voices begat, began, begin rise again and again, et encore, et encore over a frozen space that spread wide, into a long drawn ache. A sparse sparseness that stretched scarce into scared.

POÈTE:
Ils ont été greffés sur l'arbre mince des prairies
affilées au couteau du vent qui coupe le souffle.
Dans blanc d'hiver, les rafales avalent le bord des ditches!

PIONNIÈRE:
Dans cet inabordable inédit des prairies
On a subi le choc la claque du vent du blanc!
Winded by winter, by never-ending weather
by the shock of white!

POÈTE:
Après une visite aux cimétières du Nord,
mes vieux, éparpillés, me sont revenus
dans cet avenir post post modern que je vis.
Ils veulent que je raconte de quoi il s'agissait,
dans ce temps là, de quoi ils s'agitaient.

I sit on their quarter section. Sit and listen. Out of thin air, of insubstantial, j'entends un fracassement de vieux os.

PIONNIÈRES:
Chut! R'garde la, là, assise à terre. Elle écrit, Elle!

POÈTE:
J'écris sur les feuilles
fragiles des artéfacts.

In the meagre stuff
My grandparents left behind,
mere traces.
In the few artifacts
left behind–
baptismal certificates–
On Both,
the theme
of near death at birth–
I place these
Sur la patène de
mes recherches–
Thin wafers of the past,
I take and eat.

Out of these scant
time-yellowed traces,
these meagre materials,
I conjure up pieces,
the way they did
with almost nothing–
Their life.

PIONNIÈRE:
Scrapings
Every
Scrap
Used

POÈTE:
Palimpsestes:
Je gratte pour recueillir
toutes les syllables
délabrées que me soufflent
mes défunts...

Scratching the surface,
touched by the voices of my dead,
I catch glimpses
of a whole way of life–
just always scraping by.

Peau tatouée d'éraflures,
leurs mains, de gerçures.

PIONNIER:
Trop de pluie,
le creek qui déborde,
Rotten swaths, lost crops...
Pas assez de pluie.
L'eau brunie...

MÉMÈRE:
Feu de cheminée!

POÈTE:
<change of tone–speaking directly to the "grandmothers">

Je vous ai cherché partout dans vos sacs de retailles les mémères.
Comme vous j'ai enfilé mon aiguille
J'ai raccommodé les tissus usé à' corde de vos vies dures.
I patched holes, sewed 'round edges of threadbare cuffs.
J'ai reprisé avec les fils qui pendaient,
J'ai raboudiné les bouttes qui manquaient
entre vos bribes d'histoires.

J'ai brodé autour des manches râpées
pour vous, couples épuisés, effrayés
au boutte comme mes crayons,
que j'affile jusqu'à l'efface.

J'ai voulu vous faire de la dentelle,
assoupir l'amertume des mères,
vous qui aviez dû subir l'oubli de soi.

Their near erasure
from the landscape–
only a slight indent
left   in the dirt,
where their first home once stood–

a hole-in-the-ground,
creusé à' pelle,
next to a spring-flooded,
summer-sluggish creek.

MÉMÈRE:
Je n'oublierai jamais notre arrivée dans le Peavine. Y' avait mouillé pis...tout ce qu'on voyait devant nous, c'était une trail dans la bouette. Nos bœufs avançaient pas vite dans c't'e fameux gumbo. On restait stuck! Mon doux Émile a du enfin marcher avec ces pauvres bêtes, les tirailler...

PÉPÈRE:
On va y arriver Annie. Un tour de roue à la fois.

LE VENT:
Saplings, wisps in subzero, little whips in the wind.
Souches simples et affilées au couteau du vent.

PIONNIÈRES:
On plie, on prie, on rit, on se fait du fun!
On met tout ça dans les mains du Seigneur...
Sur la terre comme au ciel.

MÉMÈRE:
Dans mon île, mon Jersey à moi, l'air de la mer...
si doux pour la peau des femmes...
Ici, le froid est si sec, i' fait tout plisser la peau.
Quand j'm'r'garde dans le mirroir...J'vois une vieille, laide.

Ben, j'y retournerais pas
Mon amie Blanche m'écrit qu'astheure, y' a trop de *tourists*,
pis de jeunes qui viennent se saouler, pis danser dans les night clubs toute la nuite!
<dreamy tone as she continues>
C'était toute *natural* dans mon temps...

PIONNIÈRE:
On a dû vivre à vif
au son du métronome
de la survie.
Efface pis recommence...
Recommence

Nos hommes zombies
harnachés à la charrue,
acharnés à défricher.
à prouver le *homestead*.[3]

PIONNIERS:
WE BROKE THE LAND!
PULLED ROOTS.
PICKED ROCKS.
DRAGGED STONE BOATS.

MÉMÈRE:
C'était pas le paradis terrestre c't'e Last Best West.
Notre chaumière à plancher en terre, à toît qui nous coulaient sur la tête! Je l'appelais «La catacombe de Rome»!

En tous cas...Y'en a qui se sont sentis bluffy par le prêtre...

POÈTE:
Le couple attelé
sous un gros load
d'exigences.

PIONNIÈRES:
<Imitent la voix du Prêtre>

PIS, SOUS LES RÈGLEMENTS DE L'ÉGLISE!
RÈGLES À NE PAS MANQUER,
SOUS PEINE DE PÉCHÉS MORTELS!
NE PAS EMPÊCHER LA FAMILLE...?

PRÊTRE:
LE DEVOIR DE TOUTES LES FEMMES, C'EST DE:
RENOUVELER LE BERCEAU À TOUTES LES ANS.

---

[3] Un homestead de 160 acres coûtait $10 et le colon avait three ans pour le "prouver" (obtenir ses lettres patentes) en construisant une habitation, et en défrichant un certain nobres d'acres chaque année. Le colon devait habiter sur son homestead pendant au moins six mois par année./
A 160 acre homestead cost $10. The owner was required to prove his homestead in three years by: constructing a habitation (a shack), living in it for at least six months a year, and clearing his land for seeding.

PIONNIÈRE:
HAN?!
À cause d'un p'tit cinq minutes
de répit dans le lit.
Oopsie doopsies! Règles manquées.
Un autre baby on the way.

POÈTE:
C'était pas juste du folklore
ce qui se passait,
ou ne se passait pas
dans le lit conjugal.
du crépuscule à l'aurore

PIONNIÈRE:
D'abord, comment faire l'amour, HAN?
(change of tone, seductive, playful)
Ben, faire ses devoirs, tard le soir.
Night murmurings, sweet whisperings,
And, the two became ONE. AND: TWO. THREE. FOUR.
FIVE. SIX and TWELVE, and TWENTY-FOUR...

POÈTE:
OUI! I' fallait peupler l'Ouest. Faire des fils, des fils, en masse de fils. Pour travailler la terre! Pis des filles pour faire des bébés.
HEY BABY, BABY...BABY BOOM!

PIONNIÈRE:
Parlons-en des souvenirs du BON VIEUX TEMPS–
On était en famille tout le temps.

POÈTE:
Elles enfantaient sans soins.
Chaque fois, elles risquaient la mort.
La mortalité infantile était élevée.
Pis, les fausses couches, les morts-nés.
Enterrés au plus vite.

PIONNIÈRE:
Oublie ça! Deuils enfouis.
La vie continuait. On acceptait.
Pis, on faisait une autre batch de couches...

LE VENT:
Dans l'O infinie des prairies,
elles ont dû se perdre.

POÈTE:
J'ai verser pour vous des larmes
mes mémères morfondues.
J'ai voulu vous inventer des jeux de mots,
Des mots ailées, zèlées, des langues de feu!
Rallumer vos jouissances au pluri-ELLES!

PIONNIÈRE:
On s'occupait des tâches à n'en pus finir, on décrottait les couches, les faisaient tremper dans du bleach, les lavaient...L'eau se faisait rare dans les parages. L'hiver on rentrait d'la neige pis on allait au creek ramasser des chandelles de glace.

POÈTE:
<Comptine barbelées. To the tune of "Pat a Cake, Pat a Cake...">

Faut que les couches soient blanches.
On pense à la messe du dimanche.
Repasser chemises blanches.
Bas blancs, gants blancs.
Tous bien peignés, reluisant,
Propres et pimpants, dans notre banc.
Même si on a manqué le paiement.
Ainsi soit-il, Amen, Amen!
Le p'tit Jésus lave toutes nos peines.

PIONNIÈRE:
The Lord is my SHEPHERD
I SHALL NOT WANT...

POÈTE:
Le MUTISME installé CHEZ l'accouchante en donnant naissance.
Sans bruits, sans cris. Sans cries, now Ladies!

GOSSIPY VOIX:
Imagine-toé, en accouchant a' criait "Maman"!
Moé, en tout cas, j'en ai eu 12, puis j'ai jamais faite de scène comme ça!

PIONNIÈRE:
(weepy, in the throes of a hard birth, supplication then howls)

Sainte Marie Mère de Dieu je vous supplie! Délivrez-moi!
Maudite marde! Viarge...! Délivre-moé, CRISSE! MAMAN...!

MÈRES DES ANNÉES 1950:
Plus tard, quand on allait accoucher à l'hôpital,
le docteur nous administrait une bonne shot de Demerol...
Pis, bye-bye les labour-pains! Pis j'avais une semaine de répit, mes repas servit au lit. C'était ma seule vacance...C'tait le ciel sur la terre!

POÈTE :
MOÉ, bébé, née droguée. Vite enlevée de ma mère. Mise à la nursery. Nourrit a' bouteille par une nurse. D'la formule.

<bébé droguée, chante, baby sings a nursery rhyme in a drugged voice...>
C'est la poulette grise qui a pondu dans l'église.
Fait dodo, pis tu auras du lolo...

POÈTE:
Après l'enfantement à l'étranger,
faute d'ouverture du col de mon utérus–
Bébé en danger. Emergency. Caesarean Section!

Moé, encore droguée. Bébé enlevé.
Nuit noir s'ensuit, clouée là à mon lit.
Gorge nouée Suis tombée:
Dans la soudure des soutures.
dans la coupe de la coupure.
Absence absolue en moi, mère-tue.
Une hostie de vacance, *all right!*

De mon sein ravagé a éclaté une rage rouge
envers ce Mutisme Ultime de la Vulve,
D'OÙ LE VERBE SE FAIT CHAIR...

PIONNIÈRES:
On parlait pas d'Ça dans c'temps-là!

POÈTE:
De mon lit d'hôpital je gesticule, poings fermés,
vers ce maudit Guy in the Sky,
pis LE prêtre qui prêche dans SA chaire.
Je leurs ai glossolalié des mots mères-morfondues,
J'ai pleuré leurs chaires mal handlées, ravagées,

Leur Être in-VIE-si-bi-li-sé.
Parce qu'elles n'étaient que des femmes *fuckées*.

Y'avait des bouttes qui manquaient
dans vos histoires de devenir mère...
Des blancs de mémoire, des blancs forcés
Des maux avalés, mots ravalés, CRISSE.
Dans tout ce sang coulé CALICE.

PRÊTRE:
LE CHRIST EST MORT POUR NOS PÉCHÉS!

PIONNIÈRE:
Femmes enceintes tout le temps.
À cause de nos soi-dits péchés.
Parce qu'on faisait Ça!
PARCE QU'ON AIMAIT ÇA?

POÈTE:
Ben, fuck les règlements de l'ÉGLISE.
Le péché originel! Fuck les limbes.
Quelle mère crois ça? C't'histoire des morts-nés, pas sauvés,
enfouis dans les limbes, là, où on laisait les pas baptisés
flotter entre deux mondes pour l'éternité!

PIONNIÈRE:
Femme déviargées, nous avons été!
Entre nos jambes écartillées a coulé
de l'eau et du sang. Des enfants, en masse...

POÈTE:
Et coulera, glissera, glissera l'enfant...l'enfant...l'enfant naissant...
De nos seins, surgira du lait, du vrai...Du bleu. Vive nos règles, l'eau et le sang!

PIONNIÈRE:
En s'installant sur ces terres pour pas cher
nous les pionnières, on a dû se perdre.

MÉMÈRE:
Les maringouins! Les maringouins étaient terribles! I' nous rentraient même dans la bouche. On a appris des Cris comment faire des smudges avec du chiendent. Il fallait, pour pas s'faire manger tout rond. On sentait toujours la boucane!

PIONNIÈRE:
C'était comme ça
dans ce temps-là.
On se plaignait pas.
On pliait, on priait, on riait, on se faisait du fun!
Y' en a qui sont morte, qui non pas pu tenir le coup...

VENT:
Wisps in the wind.

PIONNIÈRES:
On se faisait du fun quand même, oui, même la nuit!
Une fois landé dans l'Ouest,
Y'avait pas à en sortir de d' là...
There was no turning back...

POÈTE:
In this Unsettling Settling
They imagined the unimaginable.
Dans cette infinitude de ciel et de terre
Elles ont vécu l'invivable!

TOUS:
Quand souffle, souffle le vent...Si l'on écoute, on entends
mille petits cœurs qui tremblent à l'unison!

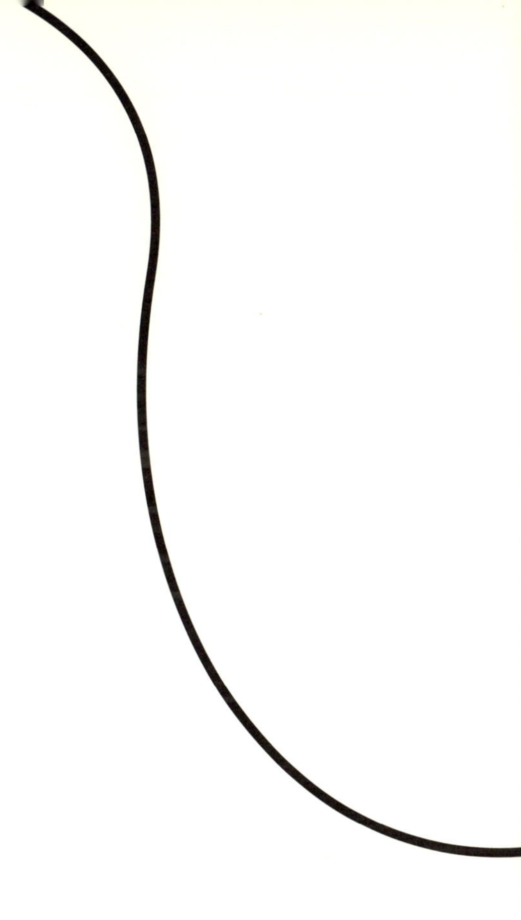

Touch in Ten Movements

by Uchechukwu Peter Umezurike

i.

Touch is memory. Bodies remember.

Imotụ aka bụ ngaghari̩. Touch is movement: my breath strains as your lips move over the ridges of my body. Skin tightens under the trail of each kiss.

Under your fingertips, I am an impala in the Serengeti.

Under your fingertips, I am a dove in a cage.

My body against yours: a gesture towards beauty. Touching is a sublime step out of my body into yours.

ii.

Is it too early for her to recoil from the body she has known for the last five years?

Chinelo is glad he can't see the look in her eyes–he can't feel her skin shrinking under his touch–his palm on her face, hers on his ass. His breath, laced with the lime from last night, sails over her face. She is glad for the darkness. Ọchịchịrị bụ ihe mgbu na-akpata. She wonders if this is how it begins–coldness–disinterest–revulsion.

iii.

The song–its slow, teasing melody–she always wanted to close her eyes and orbit in the universe of sleep, if only for a minute. The song once lulled her to sleep as they embraced each other on the floor. Outside, snow left the city pensive. The wind, full of claws and hunger. Rooftops rattled. Trees whistled.

What's that song called? Who is the artist again–the tall black guy with that lachrymal voice? Labrinth? Khalid?

This morning, as Ike drives down Métis Trail, the song comes on the radio. The fourth time he's heard it this week:

Baby, I've softened myself for you...

God knows you always touch me where it hurts.

Ike steels himself against its spell, gripping the wheel tighter. Over the hills, the sky is shale blue. Without her, he feels exposed.

iv.

I've stopped watering the anthurium. In the vase, the soil is dry and pebbly. I took you for a vibrant bloom then. Ọpupu gị
na-ewute m. But this is how I remember you–the last fading leaf.

I trace with my index finger. A heart is wilting.

v.

Touch is a poem

that nestles
between your fingers
warm and delicate

ezigbo m
smooth like the honeydew   left in the kitchen
its flesh uncut–

echoes of your laughter
the week before   we burned down
what we could no longer mend

and oh ezigbo m
the honeydew
your laughter   the flare of all our dreams

I must have been standing too long
in front of the broken mirror–   like a phantom
a scar   of a memory.

vi.

The city is a swirl of soot. Hold out your hand–powder from the sky. Hair and skin tinged with ash. We burn whatever we touch–exhale the air we have tainted with our fingers. Touch is not only where two arms meet–the pulse of intimacy. It is the scar we remember after the flame.

vii.

I have burned all our photos. I had to.

But I kept the image of you standing under the eaves of my house, face and arms lifted high, while lightning streaks the sky and the rain slides its fingers down your shoulders, all over your body, which I had longed for since we first met at our friend's soirée.

Mmiri ozuzu nke ebe ncheta. Raindrops between my fingers.

You said your father was once a priest, so you wanted to relive the childhood you never had–even if momentarily–wild and vital as the wind that night I brought you home from the bar. I was sure you shouldn't be allowed to drive home by yourself.

Yes, I burned every photograph of you–us together, the one with you standing flimsily clothed in the rain–but I have not been able to quench the burn of your touch.

viii.

"Does it hurt?" the eight-year-old girl asks, plopping beside the woman on the sofa.

The woman hesitates. Her right cheek and the inside of it still sting from the slap, which happened over an hour ago. "No, it doesn't."

"Can I touch it, then?"

The woman guides the girl's hand and lays it on her cheek. The sting seems to ease. She closes her eyes briefly, surprised darkness could feel so soothing.

The girl withdraws her hand. "Mom?"

"Yes, my dear?"

"Are we going to be all right?"

"Of course, my dear." The woman touches the inside of her cheek with the tip of her tongue.

The daughter tilts her head. "Mom? Ms. Chuki tells us not to hit anyone."

"Hmm, the lovely Ms. Chuki. She's a good teacher."

"But Dad hits you."

"Don't ever say that!" the woman says, jolted. "Your dad..." She rubs her daughter's knee. "He is dealing with things. He is...trying." She then tries to smile, but her cheek still stings. She stands up, reaching out a hand to her daughter. "Let's get you some milk and cookies."

The girl doesn't reach for it immediately. Frowning, she says, "Tochi's mom no longer lives with them. Are you going to leave me with Dad, too?"

Shame grazes the woman's skin, though she hugs the girl. "No, dear. Families stick together," she answers, wondering how long.

ix.

The woman approaches the writer as the bartender hands him another glass of wine. If only he was back in his hotel. He has had enough small talk for the night. Besides, he usually feels drained anytime he reads over 20 minutes.

"Hi," she says. "I loved your reading. You killed it. The way you conjure pictures with your words."

"Thank you," he says, touching his chest. "You're so kind."

Her hair spills golden over her cashmere scarf as she proffers a hand.

"Julie."

He takes her hand gently but briefly. "It's nice to meet you, Julie." Then he laughs. "Should I introduce myself?"

Her laughter rings around him, a surge of delight.

The writer catches a glimpse of a few guests in the room staring across at them. He sips some wine from his glass.

"What are you drinking?" The woman leans so close to him that he feels overwhelmed by her fragrance. He remembers the halved pomegranate he left in the fridge, what it smelled like.

"I can't even remember. Um, something, Chianti?"

The woman hails the bartender. "Can I please get some of what he's drinking? Thanks." She turns to the writer. "How long will you be in town for? I'd love to attend another of your readings! You have such a powerful presence." She sounds genuine.

He rubs his chin against the back of his hand. "I leave for the heart of darkness on Saturday."

She wrinkles her brow.

"Oh, I meant Congo."

"Aha! So, we can't tempt you to stay here for a few more days? You don't find our town charming enough?"

"Of course, you folks have been more than charming."

Raking her hair from her ear, she whispers, "You know, I haven't touched the hair of a Black person before."

The writer, stifling the urge to swear, stares at her. Hard. He sees her cheeks reddening.

"Sorry," the woman says. "I had a pint earlier and now...I'm sorry."

The wineglass feels colder against his palm. His grip tightens. Later, he will wonder whether the woman had something else in mind.

But now, almost scoffing, the writer says, "Honesty is rare these days."

x.

Touch is a bridge. Like trust, it can be breached. Like skin, it can be broken.

Still, it remains a span of footsteps.
Some bridges lead to freedom.

Others to misery.

Yet I don't have to touch you to know the texture of pain. That you hurt, too.

Glossary

Imetụ aka bụ ngaghari̩: Touch is movement.

Ochịchịrị bụ ihe mgbu na-akpata: Darkness is the mask that pain hides behind.

Ọpupu gị na-ewute m: I am incomplete without you.

mmiri ozuzu nke ebe ncheta: raindrops of memory

ezigbo m: my dear

ọboara: blood

TIME

Smoke

by Sana Mohsin

The sun beat down stronger that day, the middle of barren July, the day things began to pivot. Not a cloud in sight, the open bud of the sun unfurls right in the middle of the sky, heat sprawling across the Punjabi plains.

Gul wipes the sweat beginning to form high on her forehead, brings her fingers to her braided hair once to see how much it burns.

All she can really do is walk around, going along the perimeter of the haveli and then the gardens, as far as where the flowerbeds end, and the fields of wheat and greens began. Anything farther would be too far; she's bored, but not bored enough to map out the entirety of their village.

Squinting in the direction of the middle garden, she can see where her sisters are spread across two charpais. For reasons unknown, their electricity had been shut off for the day, and Gul's ears thud from the sounds of their father and his men tinkering with the power generator.

Their haveli had been built by a distant ancestor back when the British had awarded the family with land for some good colonial deed or the other. The architecture itself is straightforward enough: two floors surrounding a central courtyard, a formal dining room and drawing room, a library, a handful of bedrooms and two guestrooms, and a storeroom with a scattering of items added to by each generation. Over the years, starting likely when their family had abandoned their village for the city, the haveli had deteriorated heavily, a relic that you could pose for pictures in front of, your imagination providing all the necessary detail. At some point, their father decided that the haveli was too important to let go and spent years restoring it to the structure that stood today.

This is where they spent the summer, every summer for as long as she could remember. Their father thinks they should be familiar with their roots, with the place where their ancestors originated, even if only for a handful of months a year. The girls appreciate the thought and encourage his clinging to past days of glory even if that means their summer days would be spent waiting for them to end.

Gul, especially, does not mind. Even when there isn't any hot water, or when the radio only catches two stations, both of which played Bollywood songs so old she's never even heard of the singers. They should be the kind of family with a summer house, she thinks. It adds character.

The doors are her favourite. All of them a deep mahogany and so tall they reach the heights of the walls. Gul sees her twin emerge from the main door, her hands pushing at the etchings done on the wood by an artisan their father had specially hired. Naz holds a novel, probably even denser than the Quran, safely perched in her hands. Gogol, or some other fellow. Her fingernails are disgusting, Gul thinks, bitten to the quick even after she had applied her new midnight-blue nail polish on them.

Their parents hadn't anticipated twins. They'd selected the name Malik for a boy, a fitting name for the heir, the future master of everything, and Gulnaz for a girl, a name their mother had read in a Persian poem. When instead of the prayed-for boy two girls came out, her parents simply split the syllables of the name between them.

The heat getting to her, Gul makes her way to her sisters who had pushed the charpai toward a small patch of shade. Fizza, the oldest, is in the process of sectioning Minahil's hair so she can apply oil to it. Fizza's eyebrows are furrowed, while Minahil has her head in her lap, her hair spread out like a river. Naz is buried deep in her book.

"Why couldn't our ancestors have planted an apple orchard instead of all this wheat?" Gul announces. "We would've had some shade that way."

Fizza hums in response, and Naz doesn't look up from her book. Minahil is likely still thinking of her birthday the next day, her fifteenth. Her eyes remain closed.

Gul huffs and plops down onto the charpai, arms spread out. How many more days until September?

"I heard Papa's going to have some guests over soon," says Naz, placing a cloth bookmark in her novel. She had made it herself, one of several made during the summer they all took up stitching.

"Who?" Minahil replies, cracking open an eye to look at her.

"I'm not sure. Mama only called them the English guests."

That got Gul's attention. "Who?" she repeats.

"Maybe it's one of Papa's old university friends?" Fizza ventures, halfway through with the oiling process by then, "There's so many of them, I won't be surprised if one had moved to the U.K."

"I don't understand this whole concept of desi people moving to England," Naz exclaims, "Almost 300 years of English rule, thousands of lives lost in the Partition they mandated, only for us to work for them again? Ridiculous!" Her voice rises with every statement, her expression animated for once.

There's no use talking to her twin once she gets into one of her political moods. How can two people who virtually shared the exact same physical features be so different? That goes for all four of them really–so close in age, so similar in appearance, but living as if they're from different worlds. Sometimes, Gul wishes she was as articulate as Naz, as well-read.

But that means she'll never have any fun.

•

There's no escaping it. Wherever you go, whenever you try to hide behind a sofa or bury your head in a book, the eyes follow. Their grandfather's portrait hangs right in the centre of the living room. Of almost monstrous proportion, it is said to capture the likeness of the man perfectly. But Naz can't judge, he'd died long before she was born.

Maybe the portrait is a punishment for Papa from beyond the grave, Naz muses. Grandfather was a known misogynist, and Papa has four girls.

She's lounging on the sofa, her legs dangling off the armrest. Around Naz is chaos. A cluster of hired staff come and go, accompanied by Mama's booming voice giving out instructions. The guests are due today, and since they're foreign and apparently well-off there's a need to impress them more than usual. Mama is in the process of bringing out her best silverware, purchased from somewhere in East Asia during the beginning of her marriage, and the guest rooms are stocked with fresh linen and decorated with imported lilies on the bedside tables. Their mother is ready to fully utilize all the weapons in her arsenal tonight.

Consequently, the girls have also put on their fanciest shalwar kameez and are thoroughly lectured about being on their best behaviour. Despite the whining, secretly Naz thinks they're all thrilled, if the care with which they selected their suits is any indication. Even she's a participant, wary of strangers as she is. Naz doesn't care about the guests themselves, or how annoying it will be having to act proper while they're visiting. Something is breaking the monotony of their summer days, and this is enough for her.

"Rashid! Why isn't the okra done yet? They'll be here any minute," Mama yells at the cook.

There's Naz's reason to escape. If she stays any longer, she'd get caught in the eye of Mama's storm.

By the time she climbs the stairs to hide in her room, Naz hears the faint slam of a car door from the open windows.
"Come on! The guests have arrived," Gul calls from their shared room.

Naz prides herself on her composure, in the intelligent sensitivity that sets her apart from the rest of her sisters. But she can't fight the sharp buzzing underneath her skin, the spike of adrenaline in her blood. Naz is anticipating something that'll show its face to her soon enough.

Her sisters gather around their room's large double-door windows. Naz crosses the room, and the four girls peer outside, heads together, a jumble of wavy dark-brown hair of various lengths.

There's a boy outside their house.

From a distance he's tall and lanky, with the typical brown hair and skin. He has on an ironed white shirt and dark pants, giving off an aura of put-togetherness despite a long flight.

Papa's laughing with a balding man, presumably his friend. Naz has only recently learned he had moved to England in the '70s and became a successful businessman. The silver watch on his right wrist looks brand new, glinting like freshly struck metal, reflecting the sunlight onto his clothes. He had taken his entire family with him to England, and they'd all decided that it would be too hard to adjust back to living in Pakistan, so might as well not go at all. The girls had only expected Uncle, no mention at all of a young man accompanying him.

The boy heads towards Mama, bowing a bit so that she can place her hand on top of his hair, giving him her blessing. He greets Papa with a loud salaam, forgoing syllables, clipping the endings, almost a mockery of the word. It's evident that this family didn't speak Urdu at home.

Papa catches sight of the four of them and stops his joking to shout, "Those beauties are my daughters! Come down and say salaam to Uncle."

There's a forced smile on Papa's face, one that's confined to his lips instead of filling his whole face, one that he reserves for his business clients. Naz looks at Mama, who is fussing with her dupatta, making sure the drape falls right and doesn't crumple her suit. Uncle looks around the property, at the house, at their cars, separating a bit from the group to get a better look at the fields.

The boy looks up towards them. His eyes are golden brown in the sun. He doesn't seem to look at anyone in particular, his eyes flitting speedily across their individual features, moving far too fast to retain anything.

"Let's go," says Fizza, "or else Mama will complain."

Naz begins to trail behind her as Gul follows. Naz calls out to Minahil, who's still looking down from the window.

"In a minute," she replies, in a voice that's faraway. "He's smiling at me."

•

The extra two seats at the dinner table seem out of place, as if the balance has been skewed. As time goes on, the table struggles to keep up with the dishes laid on top of it, fulfilling the new guests' requests even if that meant having to go out of your way. And what requests they are! Out-of-season fruits and drinks that have long been discontinued. Curries cooked in the purest of ghee. The preciseness of the circumference of the rotis, the perfect ratio of butter on top of them. The inhabitants of the house wonder, is this the way to live a truly lavish life?

That night's menu is chicken tandoori, the flesh raked over burning coal, the smoke still fresh through the tendons. The elder guest sits at the head of the table, saying something about wanting to have a good look at everyone's faces. The father of the family does not complain, knowing better than to treat a guest badly.

The elder guest keeps speaking, even through mouthfuls of chicken, giving the table their own good view. Something about how he got his business set up in England, how readily the people there claimed him as their own, despite his brown skin. How great the English are, better mannered than Pakistanis. How clean the streets of London are, how well-constructed the buildings...etc., etc.

One of the twins, the one with the particularly shrewd expression, remarks that she's read that the area the guests live in has a sizeable Pakistani population.

The elder guest is offended, though he tries to play it off in a series of forced chuckles. No, no, you must be confused. Only authentic English people live in our neighbourhood. Only true Europeans.

He gets back to his story, undeterred by the minor setback.

He doesn't notice that no one seems to be listening, not even his own son, Khalil, who's much too busy sneaking looks at the youngest daughter, who in turn looks at him coyly from beneath her fan of eyelashes. The father looks toward the guest though his eyes are glossy. The mother speaks with one of the cooks to assemble dessert. The twins speak to each other through blinks and glances, in their own world. The eldest daughter looks at her reflection on her plate.

•

Fizza wakes up to a door slam. For a moment her body tenses with shock, and she listens for any accompanying, alerting sounds. When there are none, she turns over. The glow-in-the-dark hands of her bedside clock show that it's just after 2 a.m., when the whole haveli should be in deep sleep. Even Uncle. Fizza recalls his nightly stories to an audience after they were all done with dinner. He's eager to share his experiences of the advanced Western world with his underprivileged, uneducated Pakistani counterparts. Mama must shoot Naz particularly harsh glares whenever she looks ready to answer back.

Fizza gets out of bed and wraps a shawl around herself. The haveli's electricity is still faulty even after all these weeks have passed this summer, so she lights a candle to guide her way, only to find an empty hallway. The smoke rises from flame, too close to her face, so she coughs a bit. Not thinking enough to have put on her shoes, she feels the rough concrete of the floor. Next to her room is the small storage room Minahil claimed as a bedroom that year, saying something about being too old now to share with the rest of her sisters. Her door is still closed, and Fizza touches the still warm door handle, but stops herself from opening it. What if the slammed door had just been her imagination, and she'd be disturbing her youngest sister for no reason?

The thought remains with her for a second more when she notices solidifying wax on the floor. Her own candle hasn't been burning long enough for that. Bending down a bit, softly, Fizza sees more drops of wax, while the smoke from her candle forms a snake in the air. A trail.

She's led straight to the library, her heart thumping in her ears the entire way. What's she expecting exactly? A break-in? Minahil, in danger in her own home? She's being irrational.

The library door's left open just the tiniest bit. So, Fizza hears sounds.

Quiet giggling. Fizza knows the unmistakable high-pitched laughter of her youngest sister. But she also hears deeper laughter. Clothes rustling. Soft sighs.

Fizza can't take it anymore. "Minahil?" she calls, perhaps a bit too loudly in her panic, opening the door halfway.

The sounds stop, but the silence beats violently against Fizza's ears. She counts each beat.

Slowly, her sister appears from behind one of the bookcases. Fizza still can't make out Minahil's face, but her footsteps are measured, as if cautious of scaring away an animal. Behind her emerges Khalil, their other guest for the summer. He comes closer, and in the candlelight his eyes look like honey.

Minahil avoids looking at Fizza and walks away in the direction of her room. On his way out, Khalil gives Fizza a sheepish smile. She blinks at him and watches their retreating figures.

She should've known, with the looks the two have given each other across the dinner table in the first two weeks of the visit, with the way that Minahil volunteered to take Khalil on a tour of the village, even though she hated going out in the humidity.

How can Minahil be so stupid? Fizza thinks this might have been all her fault. Minahil's the baby of the family, five whole years younger than Fizza. Her heart wrenches with tenderness sometimes when she so much as looks at her youngest sister. They have an easy relationship, not competitive like the twins. The age difference between them is enough that Minahil almost respects Fizza.

These kinds of flirtations didn't harm anyone as long as they remained inconsequential. Minahil knows there're rules, curated by her older sisters from their own experience. Never in the house, where Mama and Papa were. Never with someone important, someone who the parents were aware of. Most importantly, never alone. How could they all protect each other if they didn't share secrets?

Fizza realizes she's bleeding. She's gripped her arm at some point, nails digging hard enough to break skin.

•

Minahil raises her hand to knock on Gul and Naz's door but in the next moment stops herself. She needs to think first, to plan it all out in her head. In hindsight, that's something she should've done before this whole thing started.

Stupid. Absolutely stupid. But all she could think of was how Khalil's eyes resembled the sun.

How would she even bring it up? The twins likely already knew about Khalil and her. She had caught her older sisters talking in the living room two days ago, their heads close together, and the radio so loud Muhammad Rafi's voice echoed in their haveli. They had stopped as soon as they saw her.

Honestly, they've never been good about keeping secrets from each other.

Minahil shakes her head–almost as vigorously as their security guard's German Shepherd shaking water out of his ears–attempting to rid herself of the whirlwind of her thoughts. She feels a stray tendril come out from her careful braid, but Minahil finds that she does not care enough to straighten it. She chooses to forgo knocking altogether and swings the door open. Inside she finds all three of her sisters. They had pushed Gul's and Naz's single beds together, and now lie in various languid poses, their limbs fitting around each other. Their conversation halts as she enters. Minahil finds herself getting annoyed at their now predictable reaction, but does she even deserve that? For a too-long minute, they all stare at each other. Minahil can't stand the silence.

"I'm such an idiot," she says, her voice breaking. Still, her sisters are silent, looking back at her with almost identical dark eyes. Minahil continues, tears forming in her eyes.

"It was a whole thing, I thought I'd gotten pregnant. I know I shouldn't have; I know."

It's Naz who speaks up, "Thought you were pregnant? Past tense?"

"Uh-huh. I just had this feeling you know, for the whole of last week. Worried. And then my period came."

Gul laughs at this, unkindly. But Minahil doesn't fight with her right now. Not when she needs Gul on her side.

"I told Khalil first. And he gave me this," continues Minahil, pushing back the sleeve of her shirt to show the lilac bruises that littered the length of her arm. Naz narrows her eyes, for a moment looking just like Mama when she's angriest. Fizza reaches for Minahil's hands, pulling her to sit with them on the bed. She reaches to circle her arms around her, not really a hug until Minahil crashes into her chest. The twins look at each other, something passing between them.

•

Khalil thinks the world is ending.

Growing up, he had an Indian Muslim nanny, which was his parents' attempt to keep him from becoming completely Anglicized. Instead of simple bedtime stories, the nanny would detail how the Day of Judgement would take place, and how all sinners would burn in hellfire. As a child, he was traumatized and learned to expel bad memories from his brain as he grew. Khalil doesn't know why that nanny came to mind as reality crashes around him.

He can't breathe or move any of his limbs. He's awakened in this state so can't fathom what is happening. But as he gains bearing of the situation, Khalil realizes that something holds him down. Or someone. The weight on his head lifts. Before Khalil can even think to blink, hands reach to cover his mouth with thick cloth. He looks up, the smell of smoke in their vicinity. Minahil's dark eyes are peering straight down at him, too close to his face.

"We thought you should be able to see."

Still. Enraged. It was Gul's voice. In his handful of weeks here, he has learned to differentiate the few features that subtly distinguished the sisters from each other.

Khalil's arms and legs are tied with what could only be rope. When he tries to struggle, it scratches his skin so roughly he fears the skin will peel off. Where have they learned to do this? Why is this happening?

Around him, the four sisters stand. The dimness of the candlelight throws intersecting shadows across their faces. Khalil doesn't scream until he feels something searing hot on his chest.

•

Summer is over.

No one could figure out why Khalil was so quiet for the rest of the visit. His shoulders seemed almost permanently hunched, and he spent his remaining days in his designated guestroom, soundlessly reading Dickens. Uncle blamed homesickness, for this was normal for any boy on his first trip to the supposed motherland.

Their last day as guests. Papa and Mama are at the gate to say goodbye as Khalil lifts their suitcases into the trunk, wincing. He shakes hands with Papa and thanks Mama for her hospitality. Even after everything, he can't forget his manners.

From the large double windows four sisters watched him leave, their heads together. Arms around each other, they watch the car leave, puffs of gasoline trailing behind. It's time to go back to the city.

Ripped Seams

by Giselle General

Lola Aleg, my mama's mother, brought mama's sewing machine into the store that would serve as our new home. In the main floor of the store, surrounded by shelves of various products we sold, the sewing machine was an attempt to make the space feel homey. We placed the family TV on the shelf behind the door, between bundles of colourful fabric we sold by the yard.

Downstairs under the ladder, the gas stove and the water purifier surrounded the new sink. In the bathroom stood the washing machine right next to the toilet, left unchanged after the store had been repaired. The toilet tilted backwards. The washing machine tilted sideways.

Lola had just come back from another trip. I thought she had been away for a week that time. Maybe two? The length of time that she left me and Greg was getting longer. I lost count as she was away so frequently. She never texted or called, leaving me and my brother in the dark.

When she returned this time, I noticed two sacks leaning on each other behind the door. The plastic woven sacks were the same ones used for rice and salt and held 50 kilos. But these sacks didn't look brand new. They looked like they had been washed and re-used.

I curiously eyed the sacks with the strange-looking lumps, no hint of what was inside. They were tied by a plastic rope at the top, enough to close it but not sealed tightly enough to keep grains of salt, sugar, or rice from spilling out. Whatever was inside them must be larger than those tiny grains.

She opened the sacks and pulled out an armful of clothes. The scent of moth balls assaulted my nose. "This is how you make sure that they don't get eaten by termites. See, they are still in good condition. Let's see if any of them fit you."

Amazed and confused, I looked at the clothes. Dresses and pants and blouses of varying colours and styles that I didn't recognize. She started another one of her stories.

"When your mama and all your titas and titos were younger, I made all their clothes."

I eyed the pile of clothes that spilled out of the sack. Some dresses felt silky to the touch. Some pants looked like the familiar denim but with lines that looked almost white.

“After I finished high school, we didn’t have any money, so I didn’t go to college. Instead, I went to a vocational school and learned sewing.”

She pulled out a pair of pants, the same brown colour as the cardboard boxes our groceries came in. I was surprised how soft they felt. I folded the pants and added them to the growing pile of pants, jackets, fluffy skirts, and stiff blouses that was almost toppling over.

“After that, I didn’t get a job related to sewing, but I started my business in Urdaneta City. And then I expanded from there. To Dagupan, Pozorrubio, and then here in the mining villages. Lepanto and Antamok and then in Philex.”

I stared at two jackets made of leather, fit for a movie star or a rock singer. I pictured in my mind someone like Elvis Presley on stage, shimmying while wearing the white one with leather strings along the arms. The black one would suit someone like Fernando Poe Jr. on an action movie scene while fighting the bad guys to save the day. Lola smiled as if she remembered the day she made them.

“All the clothes I made for the children; I kept them all in the house in Jenkins. So here are some of them. There’s some in your Lolo’s store here in the market area. We’ll get them too.”

She explained that with many of the dresses, she purposefully added a few inches of fabric, folded and hidden away in the seams.

A new routine began between us. I would try on a dress or a shirt, stripping off my clothes while hiding behind shelves. I peeked through the gap between the shelves in case a customer was by the counter window. We made sure customers couldn’t see me naked while I treated the back of the store like a dressing room.

There was a white dress, with a fabric that felt like cotton with a lot of holes in it, but it looked like the holes were made on purpose.

“This one, it is called eyelet, okay? This fabric is thick but of course the holes will still show your skin. See? That’s why the bodice has a lining underneath. You still have your tita’s under slip skirt I gave you, right? Wear that to cover your thighs when you wear this dress.”

There was a dress with dark blue puffed sleeves, wide skirt, and a white bodice. Wearing that dress made me feel like Snow White.

"This one fits you perfectly. We don't need to change anything. This is good! I know how messy you are though. You have to make sure you don't spill any food or drink on it. It's easy to bleach something that is all white, but not something like this."

Another dress had a white bodice, with ruffled sleeves and a skirt with purple frills that went round and round in circles. There was so much fabric that even when I lifted the skirt, fabric covered my legs completely.

"This one. This is not from your mama. I made this for one of your titas for a dance performance in school. The skirt is so fluffy, sitting on it all day might have been uncomfortable. But if it fits you and you want to wear it to school, that's fine."

Half of them were a good fit. Sometimes, even after Lola unravelled seams to find more fabric, I simply couldn't squeeze myself in. I heard about numbers and measurements all the time. She told me, "Your mama, she was 22 inches at the waist when she got married. Your tita Lanie and tita Debbie are around that size too!"

My eyes bugged out hearing this number. I thought it was unbelievable! I am quite far from 22 inches. I am 28 or 30 inches at the waist at least. And a tummy that rounds out. It's one of the many ways I will never be like my mama. My handwriting was terrible, I couldn't speak Ilocano or Pangasinense, my art was not pretty, and now, I couldn't be as slim as her.

Some of the sacks contained clothes for men. Just as with the dresses, Lola seemed to know when she made them and who she made them for.

"In the '70s this type of collar was very popular for the men. Your uncles would pick any pair of jeans they wanted from the stock, then I made polos to match. Your uncle Willie liked to play guitar, so he had many outfits for when he went out to play."

Lola must have thought that Greg felt jealous of all the clothes I was getting. But he was too small for my uncles' clothes. She had sewn brand-new clothes for my brother to wear at home instead. She made a few pairs of shorts using fabric from our stock. He still had many of his modern-looking clothes he brought back from Baguio City, so he didn't need much for going out.

On weekends when the electricity was shut off for a few hours, the store was silent except for Lola's sewing. The click-clack of the metal pedals, the humming of the leather band rolling the two wheels, and the chittering of the needle piercing through thread got interrupted only by a customer coming to the front counter saying "pabili po!"

Lola showed me a robe, a shade of green like my first pair of earrings I got from mama. White stitches curled and moved around the fabric, like a snake that didn't end. It felt puffy like a blanket that had its own sleeves and a skirt. I tried it on, and Lola looked at me with satisfaction. She said it was perfect for sleeping at night up in the attic. It was cozy and went all the way to my feet. Some buttons were missing. Lola took a few gold-coloured buttons from our stock and made me sew them on. The robe wrapped me like a cocoon every night, the only warm hug I had received in quite some time.

In school, every Wednesday was civilian clothes day. I had so many dresses that I wore a different dress every week. When I decided to go to church, I also wore a different dress each Sunday.

We didn't have a cabinet for clothes in the store. In the attic where we slept, we folded our clothes in piles and lined them up in a row along the mattress. Each of us had a corner.

As the months passed by, I noticed the clothes my classmates were wearing. I tried to wear modern clothes or older blouses and jeans more often on Wednesdays at school and reserved the dresses for Sundays. I didn't want to be made fun of for wearing clothes older than me. I hoped that God would still welcome me for wearing those very old clothes when I went to church.

Another weekend came and Lola said she would be gone for a few days. She didn't say for how long. My heart sank as I realized I was in charge of the store, all the chores, my studies, and looking after my brother again. For my pambahay outfit, unsophisticated house clothes, I picked a pair of pajamas with cartoon characters I liked. An attempt to feel more like a 10-year-old than an underage store manager.

While Lola was gone, the sewing machine was closed and tucked away. Its wood varnish matched the shelves where we stacked products to sell, not quite the homey appliance it was supposed to be. As my brother and I laboured from sunrise to sunset, we waited eagerly for Lola Aleg to return and for the chance to feel like children again.

enough to make you cry

by Rita Bouvier

(After "Elders First." [multi-channel video and sound exhibit] Part of *Time Holds All the Answers* by the arts collective Postcommodity. Exhibition September 18, 2021, to January 23, 2022. Remai Modern, Saskatoon, Saskatchewan.)

groping darkness
it is enough that ringing
repetitive in your ears
could cause deafness
        perhaps drive you to the edge
        of madness you want to leave immediately
except the images
projected on screen
        are pulling you in

kihtêyak–wise ones
caught by camera eye
appear one after the other in rapid succession
sitting alone in confined   barren spaces
        disappearing
into over-stuffed threadbare   armchairs
staring out   smudged broken windows
        into the beyond
landscapes   lush with wolf willow and wild flax

then slowly   an emerging disparity
grows before your eyes
flashes of the haves
        a stark juxtaposition   like the word itself
in their spacious rooms   plush markings of velour
soft leather sofas too many satiny throw-pillows

        still   still
they   too   sit all alone
vulnerable–in need

of all the nourishment
a physical body   a spiritual being
needs to survive this end-of-life journey

you wonder
who exploits and abuses
makes profits
from care of our mothers fathers aunts uncles
grandparents great-grandparents great-great...

that ringing in your ears
won't stop   you search for a door out
but now there's a hole in your heart
that needs mending

momentarily blinded by bright light
you lose balance   trip over your own feet
catch yourself   this time!
you leave   as you came   groping darkness

飢餓是遺傳的 Hunger is Inherited

by Kathryn 君妍 Lennon

I see my mother's mother,
squatting on a newspaper in our kitchen
her hands folding
bamboo leaf triangles around sticky rice.

I see my father's mother,
sitting by a window in a red dress
her hands unpeeling
Kraft singles.

I've gone searching for recipes
in kitchens of other grandmothers
only to find them stuck
like tea leaves to the sides
of my cup.

Until the only thing left to do
is to visit the only grandmother left.
I cross the world
to see 婆婆 Po Po.

Now, here, I sit, hoping she'll speak to me.
Hoping she'll teach me
hoping she'll spill kitchen secrets
of black beans, cornstarch, and soy sauce
brought to a boil,
thickened.

But what I learn instead:
to thicken my skin
so her words will not hurt me.

婆婆 Po Po's skin
is paper-thin, blue veins raised like
remnants of the great wall

and I wonder if her great wall
of stubbornness will ever fall.

She falls more often now,
broken both hips, hit her head.
The arched feet once planted
in the street, selling vegetables,
bok choy, gai lan, choy sum,
no longer steady her.
But she is stubborn and fear of falling
is nothing compared to fear of failing
to feed one's family.
She still remembers hunger.

She worries I'm hungry,
gets up to shuffle into the kitchen
and I follow, hoping
I will find kumquats preserved in salt
after the New Year, hoping
I will find secret maps tattooed
onto the backs of my hands,
maps that will let me
crisscross checkpoints and bypass borders
trading secrets for spices and spices for seeds.

But, the kitchen is small.
I'm too tall.
I don't know
how to hold a knife,
how much rice to cook for two,
I don't know
the names of vegetables.

She tells me, get out of the way!
From the sidelines, I watch her
rinse rice,
slice wintermelon,
heat peanut oil in wok,
crisscross green onions, ginger, soy sauce
across fish belly.

My belly has never known
hunger. Yet, I am afraid
when the last Saskatchewan farmer

yields to Monsanto
we won't know how to feed the cities.
When the grandparents are gone,
our tongues will long
for food we no longer know
how to name.
The food we eat will feed us
but our taste buds will not flower.

I am afraid to tell her why I'm here.
Afraid to say: 婆婆 Po Po, I'm hungry.
Hungry for recipes for survival
to help me hold out against the
day-to-day doubts that come from
not knowing the words to name my hunger.
Hunger for the wisdom of women who
carry the weight of the world on their hips.
Hunger, because if I have a daughter,
I don't know what colour
her skin will be or what language
she'll dream in, but
I'll need to teach her to
trust her gut,
find the food that makes her heart
and stomach fly.

But, I can't say this in Cantonese.
Luckily, I love to eat.

Now, it's six o'clock.
Fish is steamed, the neighbours are home, and the news is on.
So, I pour the tea, fill our bowls
as she shuffles out from the kitchen and takes her seat.
I turn to her and say the only thing I know how to say,
"婆婆 Po Po, 食飯 sik fan," eat rice, grandmother.

And we eat.

So We Shall Return

by Rona Altrows

Rechitzah
(physical cleansing)

Well, Loretta, I know you don't like that I went ahead with it anyway, but here I am, no regrets. If you want to sense what it's like, enter a quiet room, shut the door, close your eyes. You will pick up my sensations, you will feel the me I am now as movements through your skull. Go on, I'll wait.

Wow, you actually did it. Fifty-two years sisters and this may be the first time you've listened to me, I'm stunned.

The first step of the tahara ritual has begun. I feel the gentle pressure of a woman's hand as she swabs a moist washcloth over my skin, I can make out, from her touch, the shape of her hand. This woman has a compact frame like mine, I believe, from the smallness of the hand. Such a relief, this cleansing. I am grateful for the chevra kadisha, the sacred society, the people who take on the tasks of ritual burials. I count the voices of the chevra kadisha women working in this room. Four. I've always had an ear for voices, all those years in school choirs and singers' circles.

Hearing and touch, those are all I've got left of the physical senses, which defies reason, doesn't it, you'd think I'd have all five left or none, and if you look at it logically, even these two aren't what they were before, although I perceive them that way. So maybe I've got outofthisworld versions of hearing and touch, and only a mistaken perception that those two senses are still with me as I knew them before. Yet I am fully aware you are listening.

It's all new to me, the way I am now, what I can sense and what is beyond my ken. Can I transmit messages to other people, or only to you? I know I can get a message through to *you*, although I don't know how I know. If I understood how I knew, I would tell you, I believe in sharing information, I've always been open, though shy, and of course the library life always inclined me toward sharing. And through the years I've tried, Loretta, you know I've tried every so often, like on your birthdays and at family celebrations, I've tried to reconcile with you, to share myself with you, so we could be sisters in the true sense. I always wanted that to happen, even though all my attempts failed. I can only hear the sounds and voices in this small room where they have laid me down for this pre-burial ritual, tahara. I'm sorry I can't hear you, Loretta. I don't know why it's like that–I didn't make the rules. You'd have to ask whoever or whatever governs the outofthisworld senses of a person a few hours after death.

At this moment I wish I could grab my two outofthisworld senses and hold them close to my chest like they were living things and my mission were to save them from...from what?

Will the mind stay intact even as the physical brain decays, and will I keep the me that is me, my essence? Rabbi Gilda told me if you ask three Jews, you'll get three or maybe five opinions. What matters, she said, is how you conduct your life while you're living it, not what will happen later. I think I did okay. Not the best, whatever that might be, not that it's a contest. At least I never intentionally hurt anyone.

Now the women are reciting prayers in Hebrew, the prayers Rabbi Gilda showed me a few months ago, she said it was to give me an idea of the ritual, but being here for real is much more intense. It does feel real, this quiet place of thoughtfulness and no pain. The women of the chevra kadisha are real. If not, how could I feel it when they touch me? Oh yes, it is all real, as I shift to a new reality, before I have entirely left the one I knew as a living being. Rabbi Gilda said I would not be left alone ever until burial. Maybe that's partly to reassure me as I move through different states of reality, different ways of being. I understand only a few of the Hebrew words in the prayers, but the language is so melodic, I take it in as music. The women repeat the prayers in English, a prayer for forgiveness, a prayer for compassion. With the damp cloth, the woman with the small frame cleans my forehead, my nose, my cheeks and chin and neck. Every movement I receive as a touch of kindness.

Finally, I can relax, knowing I don't need any more medical assistance. Toward the end, shrunken in body and blotchy of face, I was mostly out of my right mind with painkillers, and I emitted a sickening chemical smell. It reminded me of when we were teens, Loretta, the smell of the liquid you used to take the polish off your ridiculously long nails, more like talons.

In the last days, those nurses and doctors, how they cared, they tried so hard to comfort me, to ease the suffering, to help me feel no pain. But altruism creates expectations. What if some pain remained? I decided not to tell them, didn't want to disappoint. Here, it's different. The women who wash me and say the prayers, they care too, I feel it in the tenderness of their touch, I hear it in the timbre of their voices, but they provide a different kind of care, there is no pain to stem, and they expect nothing from me.

I'll bet you think that me being here means you lost a game, everything has always been a competition for you, Loretta, but for my part I don't feel like I beat you at anything, I'm just happy to have no more surgeries, infections, complications. Nothing hurts now that I am freed from the body. There is only now. The feel of the moist cloth on my right arm, right hand, what's left of my abdomen, my vagina, my right leg. The women keep me covered with sheets as much as they can. Rabbi Gilda said that would happen, it's about treating the mehta, the body of the deceased, with respect. Aside from saying the prayers they don't speak a lot, only words they need to coordinate their work.

I always went for quiet, never wanted to fight, the slightest pressure upset me. You were the one with drive, the high flyer. Over the years, you tried to provoke me, so many times you asked how I could stand my job at the public library, sorting and shelving books. You called it grunt work, you would tell people your sister Sandy had no ambition. You said it to my face too. You, the macher, the big shot, the chief actuary at your company. I guess you thought you had the right to say whatever you wanted to me, never mind if it hurt. I told you not everyone needs to rise to the top, I told you I loved my job. I handled the library's collection every day and what could feel better than that. I mean, think of it, Loretta, maybe this is one reason you are getting my message today through your headbone. I got my hands on every single book I shelved, each one had its own texture and weight and smell. The old ones, delicate, like a person who could fall and break a bone unless I handled them with tender care. The bestsellers too, I needed to pick them up mindfully, I could see the poor things aging before their time, their spines getting sore as they passed through so many hands, they were in such demand, so busy getting their pages constantly turned, sometimes I wished they would slow down for their own sake, put themselves temporarily out of circulation. The kids' picture books with their colourful covers, just by picking those books up, I could feel the raw energy of the writers and illustrators.

My co-workers were so kind to me when I got too sick to work, they visited me often, they brought me treats and gag gifts and library stories that made me laugh. They hugged me. I am talking real hugs. They would throw their arms around me and make me feel like I was the most important person who'd ever lived. I don't think you understand displays of affection like that, Loretta.

I've never understood your disdain for me. For as far back as I can remember you have held me in contempt. But why? My friends when we were kids, and later my adult friends, noticed your coldness to me, your nonstop criticism when I was in your presence. Some of my friends are close to their sisters, so why your coldness to me? They didn't get it, Loretta, and neither do I.

Now the women turn me over gently, what a liberation, for the first time in two years I feel no pain with this movement. They wash the left side of my head, neck, arms, and go all the way down, like they did on the right side. Symmetry. I feel them pull the cover sheet off me gently as they say the vaya'an vayomer, the prayer for uncovering.

Tahara
(purification–ritual pouring of water)

I heard the women pouring water into buckets earlier. I think it will refresh me. This is tahara, the second step of the whole tahara ritual.

You know, Loretta, our mother shouldn't have put you in charge after school when we were kids and she had to be at work, you eleven and me nine, and me with a tiny frame, not like you. Big for your age. Mom didn't know I was scared to speak up, afraid of you. You yanked me by the arm as I sat at the kitchen table doing homework. Grabbed me by one wrist, dragged me down the hall to the living room and spun me over your head, your grip on my wrist so tight I thought I'd pass out. My arm felt ready to detach at the shoulder, I was dizzy and kept crying, begging you to let go. But you didn't, not until you got bored, then you'd slow the spin, finally end it, and let me down, me sore all over. Disoriented, I often would crumple into a foetal position on the carpet.

By the time we grew up we weren't close, how could we be? It wasn't like we had personality transplants. It was only when I was diagnosed, at 49, that I called to let you know. The doctors hadn't minced words on the prognosis, and you being my only living relative, I thought I ought to tell you I had a couple of years at most. You met me for coffee and actually did give me a hug, I know how you like to be the best at everything, but that was not an award-winning hug. You kept your distance, as if I were dying of a contagious disease, you placed your hands lightly on the backs of my shoulders. It's odd how a touch can be light and still not feel gentle. I've never been like you. I could always feel the intention behind a touch. You asked me what I intended for practical arrangements, and I told you what I was thinking of doing, looking into the Jewish traditions. You hammered me for the next three years trying to make me change my mind and you knew you'd get your way, because you were still older than me, still bigger, still the one to be listened to. Did you put up resistance to show you were the boss of me, like you tried to do when we were kids? There was no point then, Loretta, even as a child, even as I cringed, on the inside I had my own free self. And there was no point all those years later, as my death drew near, because I still had autonomy, in spite of your efforts to take it away. What a waste, my sister, in our early years, and our adult years and even as I died.

As my time drew closer you came to see me a few times while I was still in my right mind, not drugged up most of the time to deal with the stupid pain, and I said that yes, I had decided for sure to go with the death rituals, they sounded soothing. You told me that I couldn't do that, our family had never been observant, it wasn't as if you and I had gone to synagogue, we had not had bat mitzvahs, we had never learned Hebrew except for a few words here and there. You said I mustn't be a hypocrite, I *must* have a non-religious funeral and non-religious procedures done before burial. That's what you called how my freshly dead body would get treated, you said I'd have *procedures*. I said, I don't want those procedures, I want the traditional rituals. I swear, sick as I was, you almost slapped me in the face again, like you had done so many times when we were kids. You raised your hand, I imagined the sting of the slap on my cheek to ready myself for the real thing. I closed my eyes tight and that brought you back to your senses, or at least enough that you put the hand down. But you were still hot, you started to yell, then and there you yelled at me, a terminal patient. I was embarrassed for you. Why did you object so strongly? The religion means nothing to you one way or the other. Was it just out of spite, just to have the satisfaction of depriving me of what I wanted? It feels that way.

You didn't expect me to stick with my plan, you thought for sure I would buckle.

They are ready, they have started to pour the warm water on me, all over me, starting from my head and then all the way down, I can feel the dirt, the shmutz, being washed away, and the mental schmutz too. At the end they say, T'horah hi, she is pure.

That's the end of the tahara part of tahara. But the ritual is not quite done, nor is the story of our story, the story of you and me. Not yet.

Halbashah
(dressing in white garments and shrouds)

I had done a bit of research since the diagnosis and, a year ago, while I still had time to schlep myself around, even though not too comfortably, I arranged a meeting with a rabbi who a few people had recommended I talk to. Of course, I was nervous to meet Rabbi Gilda, it wasn't like I met a rabbi every day, but she put out her hand and took mine in more of a friendly squeeze than a handshake, such a reassuring touch. She was easy to talk to.

I said, I'm still driving myself around and whatnot, but trust me, I'm on the way out. I told her I wanted the Jewish death rituals, especially tahara. It felt important, could she help me make it happen?

I'd had multi-scenario fantasies about this moment. In one scenario she sent me away without another word, in another she said she'd think about it, but chances were slim. The reality was the opposite. Of course, she said, of course she would help me arrange for the rituals I wanted. I said to her, wait, let me tell you where I'm coming from and maybe you will change your mind. I don't remember when I last went to a service in any kind of synagogue, a shul, or a temple. And, I said, to be completely honest, I'm Jewish, yes, I always will be, but as far as belief goes, some days I'm agnostic and most days, an atheist. I'd been afraid Rabbi Gilda would recoil when I told her, but that did not happen. She smiled and said, take a number, so many of us are searchers, we question all beliefs including our own, and thank you for your honesty, you deserve the best when you die, regardless. We believe in kavod hamet, honouring the dead.

And so, Loretta, I, your sister Sandy who never talked back, I am being taken care of in the tahara room. Reconcile yourself to that fact or not, that's up to you. Now, handling my body gently and respectfully, as they have all the way through, the women dress me in the tachrichim, the plain white cloth outfit everyone gets so that class distinctions are not made. The shirt, the pants, the belt, the head covering. They lift me onto the white sheet in the aron, the coffin, wrap that sheet around me and close the lid.

So far, the touchlike and hearinglike senses are still with me, also the mind. I feel calm, ready to go on to the next stage. I will figure out what's what when that comes. I'm not afraid anymore. What about you, how are you doing? I hope you'll be at the service. It'll be quiet, like me. If you go you will feel warmth in the air, my friends from the library will be there and I trust Rabbi Gilda to give a meaningful eulogy, we got to know each other well.

Then at the cemetery, they'll lower me down into the hole. If I still have hearing and touch, I will feel the descent, and I will hear the damn creak of the winch, oh that may be hard to listen to, that's the part where I broke down when Mom died all those years back. It's not a sound you forget. If you come to the graveside, you will feel warmth there too.

And I want you to feel a surge of relaxing warmth from me now, Loretta, first in your head and then running down your body. I would like for you to feel lighter and less encumbered, like I do, my bitterness washed away by tahara. I forgive you. I forgive you for all of it.

Main Sources

1. The title is inspired by Ecclesiastes 3:20: "As we come forth, so we shall return."

2. A General Outline of Tahara Procedures, Kehillah. Accessed 21 December 2023. https://kehillahsynagogue.org

3. Guide to Jewish Customs Regarding Death and Mourning, Temple Sholom, Monticello, NY, compiled by Rabbi Michele Brand Medwin. Accessed December 21, 2023. https://templesholomny.org

4. Toward a Gender-Inclusive Hevra Kadisha, Keshet-For LGBTQ Equality in Jewish Life. Accessed 21 December 2023. https://www.keshetonline.org

About the Authors

Rona Altrows

Rona Altrows writes fiction, essays, plays, and hybrid works. Her three books of short fiction are *A Run on Hose*, which won the City of Calgary W.O. Mitchell Book Prize, *Key in Lock*, and *At This Juncture*, which won the 2020 silver IPPY award for best regional fiction. Her short stories and essays have appeared in many print and digital magazines, most recently *Prairie Journal of Canadian Literature* (Issue 80, fall 2023), *Queen's Quarterly* (Spring 2023), and *Isele Magazine* (December 2022). Rona is also a freelance editor of books and shorter works. She has edited and co-edited anthologies, including *You Look Good for Your Age*, which explores ageism against women. She is co-producer of *Gimme 10 Minutes*, afternoons of 10-minute plays, which will partner with the Calgary Public Library for its 2024 shows.

Rita Bouvier

Rita Bouvier is a Métis writer, editor and retired educator. Her fourth book of poetry, *a beautiful rebellion*, was released April 2023 by Thistledown Press. Rita's poetry has appeared in literary anthologies and journals, musicals, and television productions, and has been translated into Spanish, German, and Cree-Michif of her home community of sakitawak–Île-à-la-Crosse, Saskatchewan, Canada, situated on the historic trading and meeting grounds of Cree and Dene people (Treaty 10). Rita lives in Saskatoon, Saskatchewan, Canada.

Giselle General

Giselle General is a Filipino-Canadian artist who has called Edmonton her home since 2008. Her artistic expression ranges from creative nonfiction such as essays, anthologies, articles and blogs, to upcycled mixed media visual art. Giselle is currently developing her debut memoir, *Living on a Cliff's Edge*, that narrates her experiences, from being orphaned as a child to her immigration to Canada. She is also an emerging documentary producer, working on her first local documentary about Edmonton's Filipino community and their journey to establish a community centre. Her works have been published by CBC's First Person series, Edmonton Heritage Council's *Edmonton City as Museum Project*, numerous anthologies documenting Canadian immigrant stories, and the *Alberta Filipino Journal* as a monthly columnist since 2017.

Kathryn 君妍 Lennon

Kathryn **君妍** Lennon is a writer and editor, born and raised in Edmonton/Amiskwacîwâskahikan, with mixed Hong-Kong Cantonese and Irish ancestry. Her poetry has been published in *Canthius*, *The Polyglot* magazine, *Living Hyphen*, *The Globe and Mail*, *Ricepaper Magazine*, and the *Ethnic Aisle*. Her work has been included in several anthologies including: *Reimagining Fire: The Future of Energy* (Durvile & UpRoute) and *Back Where I Came From* (Book*hug Press).

Her nonfiction has been published in *Spacing* magazine and *Alternatives Journal*, and on *Terra Informa* (CJSR-FM). She is the co-founder and co-editor of *Hungry* zine, a food-focused publication that centres voices missing in mainstream food media. She was a member of Edmonton's 2012 Slam Poetry Team. Her collaborative poem-films have screened at the 2010 Toronto Reel Asian International Film Festival and the 2018 Bozeman International Film Festival.

Her work has been supported by the Edmonton Arts Council and the Banff Centre for Arts and Creativity (Emerging Writers Residency 2023).

Medgine Mathurin

Haitian-born spoken word artist and advocate Medgine Mathurin is a person for whom the love of language and the alchemy of words is second nature. Her multilingual upbringing (French, Creole, English) not only prompted her to begin experimenting with the potential and magic of language, but naturally compelled her into a deep love of poetry. She has been featured on CBC and Global TV, and in the Skirtsafire Festival and the Edmonton Poetry Festival. Medgine was selected as a participant in the 2022 Mentorship Program with the Writers' Guild of Alberta and became a mentor with the 2022 Horizon Writers Circle, a writing mentorship program for Black, Indigenous, and People of Colour (BIPOC), ESL, and underrepresented writers living in Edmonton. Medgine recently received the 2023 Edmonton Artist Trust Fund award from the Edmonton Arts Council and the Edmonton Community Foundation, awarded to exceptional local artists to devote time to their artistic career and encouraging them to stay in our community.

She is the author of *Waiting in the Land of the Living/Attendre dans le monde des vivants*, a chapbook published by *The Polyglot*, a multilingual poetry collection that touches on navigating chronic illness, inter-generational healing, and the wrestle of waiting for answered prayers. You can follow her at medgine.ca

Sana Mohsin

Sana Mohsin received her undergraduate degree at the University of Toronto and her graduate degree from York University. Her work has been published in *Acta Victoriana*, the *Hart House Review*, the Decameron Writing Series, and more. Her debut chapbook, *Grief Grows Elsewhere*, was published by The Soap Box Press in 2022. She is the recipient of the 2023 ZHR Writing Prize for Women for her short story "Rabbits."

Pierrette Requier

Pierrette Requier is an award-winning bilingual writer, a poet, a playwright, a workshop designer and facilitator, a mentor, and a translator. She served as the literary representative of RAFA (Regroupement artistique francophone de l'Alberta) and on the board of the Edmonton Poetry Festival as Programming Committee member, eventually creating liaisons between the French and English literary communities. She organized and hosted the first francophone Soirée poétique, French Twist, a poetry event that ran for nine years, which featured francophone talent from across Alberta. Pierrette's contribution and dedication to the diverse Alberta literary community spans over two decades. As Edmonton's sixth poet laureate (2015-2017), she not only acted as event organizer and as the host of bilingual and multilingual events and as mentor of performers, she also wrote and performed commissions for various occasions, two of which appear in permanent collections. She presented in schools (grades 2-12), in universities, at various fundraisers, and at the invitation of various organizations such as Alberta's Emerald Foundation. She has appeared at various literary festivals across Canada. In 2022, nominated by the Writers' Guild of Alberta, she was granted the Queen's Platinum Jubilee Award for her bilingual work as poet, mentor, and literary community builder.

Catalina Morales Velez

Catalina Morales Velez is a fiction and creative nonfiction writer who lives and works in Edmonton, Alberta. A native of Colombia, she depicts in her work magical elements with realistic settings, creating metaphors for the challenges she explores–such as the immigrant experience and the struggles faced by women.

Fueled by a childhood love for stories, she turned that passion into a career. Her bachelor's degree in communications from North Catholic University (Universidad Catolica del Norte) provided the foundation. She further honed her skills with diplomas in Marketing and Advertising from Colombian institutions (University Institution Esumer and Arts Institute), all while deepening her understanding of communication in urban settings with a graduate diploma from UPB (Universidad Pontificia Bolivariana).

Catalina's work has been featured in magazines in Colombia, Canada, and the U.S., including *Entrepreneur*, *Life As A Human*, *The Polyglot*, and *Revista Cronopio*.

Sandro Silva

Sandro Silva is a Brazilian-Canadian filmmaker and the co-founder of Dona Ana Films & Multimedia. He was a local producer for many international productions in his home country of Brazil, including for projects surrounding the 2014 FIFA World Cup and Rio 2016. He has produced award-winning documentaries, including *3 Siblings* (2018). After moving to Canada, Sandro wrote, directed, and produced various documentary shorts for CBC's Creator Network. He was selected protégé for the 2021 Own Voices Alberta, designed by the Alexandra Writers' Centre Society in partnership with the Writers' Guild of Alberta. He was part of the 2021 Hot Docs DOC Accelerator program, and he was selected for the 2023 Hot Docs Podcast Creators Lab. Sandro received a production grant as part of the Telus STORYHIVE 2021 Black Creators Edition, where he wrote, directed, and produced his latest documentary short, *Retraining the Brain* (2023). Sandro is working on a memoir and has several podcasts and feature documentary projects in production. Before working in the arts, Sandro worked as a copyright lawyer in São Paulo.

Uchechukwu Peter Umezurike

Uchechukwu Peter Umezurike is an assistant professor in the Department of English, University of Calgary, Canada, and the 2021 winner of the Nigeria Prize for Literary Criticism. His teaching and research interests include African and African Diaspora literatures, postcolonial literatures, gender and sexuality, cultural studies, and creative writing. His critical works have been published in journals such as *Metacritic*, *Men and Masculinities*, *Journal of African Cultural Studies*, and *Postcolonial Text*, amongst others. An award-winning creative writer, Umezurike is the author of literary works such as *there's more* (2023), *Double Wahala, Double Trouble* (2021), *Wish Maker* (2021), and a co-editor of *Wreaths for a Wayfarer* (2020).

Jumoke Verissimo

Jumoke Verissimo is an assistant professor in the Department of English at Toronto Metropolitan University. She teaches and researches in the areas of creative writing (poetry, fiction, and nonfiction). Her scholarship also extends to African literary criticism and literature, memory studies, traumatic affect, and research-creation. Jumoke has published two poetry collections (*I am memory* and *The Birth of Illusion*), a novel *(A Small Silence)*, and a children's book (*Aduke and the Moon's Hidden Secret*), which she also translated into Yoruba. She is co-editor of *Sòròsókè*, a collection of poems on police brutality in Nigeria.

Her works have been widely anthologized and translated into several languages. Dr. Verissimo's creative writing has received honours from the Edinburgh Festival First Book Award (shortlist), RSL Ondaatje Prize (shortlist), Aidoo-Snyder Book Prize (winner), among several others.

Dr. Verissimo holds a PhD in English from the University of Alberta, an MA in Performance Studies from the University of Ibadan, and a BA in Literature in English from the Lagos State University. She is currently working on a novel.